"If you think you can...
or you think you can't...
you're right."

—Henry Ford

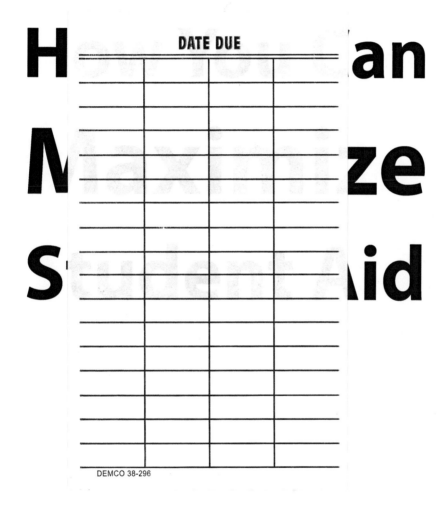

H   **an**

M   **ze**

S   **id**

DATE DUE

How You Can Maximize Student Aid

Strategies for the FAFSA and the
Expected Family Contribution (EFC)
To Increase Financial Aid for College

TRACY FOOTE
TracyTrends
New York, USA

No Substitute For Professional Guidance

This book is to be used as a starting point to understand the components involved in the computation of the Expected Family Contribution, the figure used to determine student *need-based* aid for college expenses.

Every effort has been made to ensure all references are current as of the printing date. However, information in this book is not a substitute for informed professional guidance on tax, investment, accounting, legal, or any other type of specialized advice.

This book is sold with the understanding that you will not hold the author or publisher liable for any losses, damages, or alleged losses or damages attributed from the information within and that you will seek professional assistance appropriate for your unique circumstances. One should understand the difference between information and advice, with the latter being a recommendation for actions to take after considering one's particular situation. This book is intended for informational purposes only.

Printed in the United States of America
Text Copyright © 2011, 2012, 2014 by Tracy Foote
Illustration Copyright © 2011, 2012, 2014 by Tracy Foote
Published by TracyTrends
http://www.TracyTrends.com

Please send all inquiries to:
TracyTrends
c/o T. Foote
27 West 86 St., Suite 17B
New York, NY 10024
tracytrends@aol.com

ISBN 10: 0-9814737-4-1
ISBN 13: 978-0-9814737-4-1
Library of Congress Control Number: 2011900004
Connect on social networks, comment on our articles, or subscribe at:
http://www.KidsandMoneyToday.com/subscribe

Summary of Contents

Contents

Preface

Parenting. That's what they call it on TV and in the papers. The word can be used in almost any situation. When the complaints begin, I will state to my children that I am *parenting*. It's my job.

Junior year has begun. My summer goal to have my daughter begin exploring colleges, begin drafting essays, begin something — any step toward the college process, has fallen short. Disappointed at our lack of productivity, I resolve to do better.

We will dedicate one hour a weekend to learn about colleges, to explore possibilities, requirements, and deadlines.

Reading the fine printed nine-page school listing, titled *Scholarship Opportunities*, I find the *Hoosier Heroes Scholarship*. It requires writing an essay on your Indiana hero. There are several hero categories, and you can even apply in both junior and senior year.

This will be perfect. My daughter has won awards for writing. She will be a competitive candidate. I'm pleased at how easy this is — to get started on this college process thing.

When I share my findings with my daughter, she answers with, "I'm not applying for that scholarship. Are we done?"

I begin parenting. I take control. I explain she must have a draft essay before going out next weekend. I know this is a good step because it will at least get her thinking about college.

Friday I receive her essay, a sheet of paper three paragraphs long. Prior winning essays ranged from two to six pages, but I hold my tongue. At least she wrote something. She did do something.

Next time though, I will require a certain number of words.

I begin reading. She chose her aunt, who lives in Indiana and is a professor "who influences people in psychology." Psychology? (I smile. Her aunt teaches Sociology. This is an easy fix.)

Then the essay competing for an Indiana Hoosier scholarship ends with:

> "Although Hoosiers may be seen as boring old farmers with no lives, my aunt has influenced many people in Indiana, including me and that is why she is my Hoosier Hero."

I actually stop breathing for a second, but I decide to try a positive approach. I tell her I like the idea of using her aunt, like how she included the adoption of her cousin from Jordan, and maybe she can expand on that since the essay certainly needs to be longer.

There is no comment, so I continue, "I'm not so sure about the last line, especially since it *is* being judged by people in Indiana."

She laughs.

Irritated, I try one more time, "Well, since we did move here in the past few years, maybe you could do a twist on that idea; something about how you expected Indiana to be one way, but were surprised to find it was different."

She responds now, ranting on about how she's not doing this scholarship, and tops it off with "When I need your help, I'll let you know."

I begin to lose it too, "Just how many Indiana farmers do you actually know?"

She walks out, but I raise my voice a touch louder, just to be sure she can hear, "Can you even name one?"

*   *   *

My daughter tells me she knows which colleges she will apply to. They must offer a double major, in writing and fashion design. (This is no surprise. She has been selling purses and sewing clothes since sixth grade.) She announces there are only five schools like this in the entire country. I jot down the names.

When she is at school, I contemplate visiting one during fall break. I find sights to see (so her siblings won't be bored) and hotels within our budget. This school is not my first choice, but I remind myself she is going to college—not me.

About a week later, after I've spent numerous hours Googling, I share my excitement with her about my plans for fall break.

She dismissively shakes her head, "I'm not applying there anymore."

When I ask where she will be applying, she says, "I'm going to Central Saint Martins College of Art and Design in London." There is a pause, and then she justifies the decision, "It's the best fashion school in the world."

I have no response. All I really heard was London. My mind is wondering if federal aid can even be used at overseas schools.

*   *   *

I know I can't force my child to write a quality essay in a timely fashion, but I do have some control. Instead of focusing on college acceptance, I will take the back door approach and focus on how college will be paid for. Finite numbers are a much better approach. No more wasted time on teenage indecision.

*   *   *

Focusing on finances has its frustrations as well. I was raised to believe parents prepare their children for college, but the children are the ones financially responsible for college. I thought I raised my children on this philosophy, but recently I've questioned how much of this idea has actually registered.

When I attempt to discuss college costs, my daughter tells me, "I'll just take a loan." I wonder who will give her a loan with no job or collateral. I suspect it might be me, taking that loan.

I did raise this confident child. I always said to never let money stop you from achieving your goals, but I'm becoming concerned. This may have translated to, "Mom will foot the bill."

Research shows the Federal Government is on my daughter's side. The government will actually compute an expected parent contribution toward college costs.

"Thanks Uncle Sam, I really wanted that help."

I envision my daughter will soon tell me exactly how much I am "supposed" to pay.

Delving into the rules on aid, I found I could have chosen better places to save for college, but I also found areas where there was still time to make changes that would increase our aid.

This book explains the components that determine aid, the better places to save, and what to think about come tax time. The goal is to maximize aid while keeping assets accessible, growing with tax benefits. As a valuable reference guide, it will help you prioritize, whether you are saving for a newborn or if college is looming just around the corner.

This is all part of parenting.

FAFSA Changes, Business Tips, and More

Congressional legislation continues to impact the amount of federal student aid offered and the education tax benefits. Choose your favorite way to receive notifications of recent changes:

Receive Articles:

Subscribe at: http://KidsAndMoneyToday.com/subscribe

Connect with us:

Facebook:
Click like at: http://Facebook.com/KidsAndMoneyToday

Twitter
Follow at: http://Twitter.com/KidsMoneyToday

YouTube
Subscribe at: http://Youtube.com/KidsAndMoneyToday

Google+: Follow at
https://plus.google.com/+Kidsandmoneytoday/posts

Book Updates
View updates to this book at:
http://www.kidsandmoneytoday.com/FAFSA-Education/

Review Request

If you would recommend this book to others, please consider writing a 5 star review on Amazon.com. Your time and comments are appreciated.

What's in Your Wallet?

The Federal Government will compute exactly how much parents are expected to contribute toward college. Parents cannot be forced to pay this amount, and when they choose not to, the student will have to make up the difference.

What may surprise students is the government will also compute exactly how much a student is expected to contribute.

I had trouble finding something that would explain how the current Free Application for Federal Student Aid (FAFSA) actually worked (beyond the instructions on how to complete the blanks). I wanted to know the impact of stating each financial account, the impact of the number in my household, and much more.

The FAFSA is completed in January, but the fall is when students have to decide on which schools they will spend $50 to $80 or even more for applications and related fees. How can students choose a school when they don't know how much aid will be offered? And, why would students apply to a school without knowing if they could afford it?

But, this is exactly what happens (except for the wealthy who know they can afford the full tuition).

This is equivalent to sending students shopping without explaining how much money is in their wallets. The wallet amount includes family income and assets, scholarships, grants, work-study offers, and so forth. This does not become known until spring when the student receives the acceptance package which contains the offer of aid.

This conflicts with all my financial beliefs. As parents, we aim to teach our children to be financially responsible; don't spend what you don't have. Yet, when college approaches, we will spend money on applications in the fall, yet wait until the spring, to review the financial aid acceptance package, and then, determine if the school is actually affordable.

In the spring, the student finds out, "Hey, they offered me a scholarship! I can go," or "They offered me aid, but it's a loan, not a scholarship, so I actually have to pay anyway... but at least, I got in, right?"

Right? Yeah, maybe. But, maybe Mom and Dad say, "No, not right. We're scratching that school off the list."

Why do we let students apply to schools with little idea of whether the schools are affordable?

One reason is hope. We want students to dream of attending their first choice school and to apply for scholarships in the hope of receiving them. The number one statement, "Study hard, get good grades, and you can go to whatever college you want," often made to students by parents, teachers, and mentors is, in many cases inaccurate. What we really mean is you can go to college, but not necessarily whatever college you choose.

The second reason is we are told not to rule out an expensive school. The federal formula is computed so students can consider a school they might think is financially out of their reach.

> *Example:* Suppose the federal formula states a family (parents and student) should contribute $7,000 toward college. If a school costs $10,000, the student, theoretically should receive $3,000 in *need-based* aid. If another school costs $20,000, the student, theoretically should receive $13,000 in need-based aid.

This sounds great. Based on this concept, students should be able to apply anywhere. The problem arises when aid is offered in a form of a loan. A loan is not aid. A loan is a temporary fix to an immediate problem. The college expense bill remains and eventually *must* be paid.

This book will help you make an educated guess at how much is in your family's wallet to pay for college. Included are explanations of the federal formula and strategies to reduce the amount parents and students are expected to contribute toward college expenses.

Later, you'll find descriptions of different financial accounts that have potential for tax-deferred or tax-free growth, and special rules that apply when used for education. Lastly, you'll find an overview of how education expenses impact taxes. The focus of all three areas is to keep personal funds in your own pocket.

This book should remove concerns about affording a college education. The goal is to maximize aid received, while keeping your assets accessible, growing either tax-deferred or tax-free.

A mistake on the FAFSA can result in loss of several thousands of dollars in aid, so it's crucial to obtain guidance tailored to your specific circumstances.

Not Even in College Yet

Again and again you will hear about the cost of college, but there are costs to consider even before attending school, some that may even start freshman year of high school:

1. Will your student take Advanced Placement (AP) classes? These offer a test for a fee of $89 (need-based reductions are available) and there is a $15 charge per college to send student scores. AP classes can begin in 9th grade and some students might take six or more classes by graduation.

2. How many honor societies or clubs will your student spend membership fees on, just to list on applications?

3. Will you purchase books about finding a college, paying for a college, or scholarships available?

4. Will your student take an ACT or SAT prep course or purchase practice books?

5. Will your student take both the ACT and SAT and how many times?

6. Will your student take SAT Subject tests?

7. Does your student need a medical physical to qualify for a college sport?

8. Will your family hire a college or financial advisor?

9. Will you travel for college interviews or to visit?

10. What will it cost to send ACT, SAT and/or Subject Tests scores, college applications, and school transcripts?

11. Will money be set aside for faxing additional information?

Two applications used to apply to college are the Universal College Application[1] and the Common College Application.[2] Both websites allow students to consolidate information in one location and apply to several colleges at once, thus saving the student a significant amount of time.

---

1. Universal College Application, https://www.universalcollegeapp.com/
2. The Common Application, https://www.commonapp.org/

Ask For a Waiver

It's time to start speaking up and ask for a waiver. Usually they are for lower income families, but it can't hurt to ask. Sometimes you can obtain a waiver just by stating the fee is too high for your family, without having to provide any justification at all.

Ask for a waiver or reduced fee for:

1. Annual book or lab fees

2. Honor Society fees

3. Club fees

4. The Advanced Placement (AP) tests

5. The ACT, SAT and Subject Test fees

6. College application fees

Your Calendar: From High School to College

You can plan ahead when you have a general idea of upcoming expenses. A typical student's college process calendar might be:

1. During high school years: Take AP classes

2. Estimate your Expected Family Contribution (EFC) on an annual basis beginning with freshman year of high school and obtain advice about influencing this figure.

3. Complete most strategic moves for student aid by December 31 of the junior year of high school.

4. Fall of high school senior year: Apply to colleges

5. January of senior year - Complete the Free Application for Federal Student Aid (FAFSA) and any other financial aid forms required by schools

6. February: Review the Student Aid Report (SAR) which contains your EFC. Make any needed FAFSA corrections.

7. March through April: Receive acceptance letters and evaluate aid offers

8. May: Accept a school offer

9. August: Make final college payments and begin financial planning and scholarship searches for the next year.

The Student Aid Process

While students apply to colleges in the fall, the Free Application for Federal Student Aid (FAFSA) isn't completed until January. One reason for this is the FAFSA requires reporting the family's income for the entire prior calendar year.

Ideally, tax returns should be filed before signing the FAFSA. If the return cannot be completed, estimated figures may be used, but they must be corrected later when exact figures are known. There is a verification check to match FAFSA income information with IRS tax filings.

The flow of the FAFSA information is:

1. You submit the FAFSA.

2. The FAFSA information generates an Expected Family Contribution (EFC), a Student Aid Report (SAR) and the Individual Student Information Record (ISIR).

3. The school subtracts the EFC from the Cost of Attendance (COA) to determine the student's financial need.

4. Colleges notify students of acceptance and aid offered.

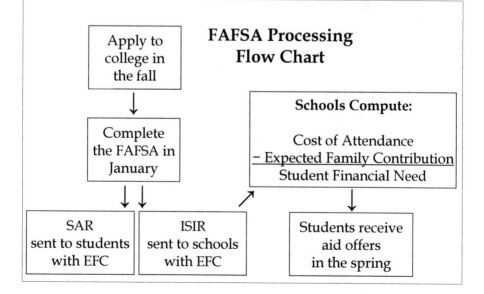

Discretionary Money

Federal aid is *need-based*. This means the greater the student's need, the greater the aid that is offered.

The formula for financial aid assumes all households have income, assets, and living expenses and once these expenses are paid, the remaining funds are discretionary and available to be used to pay for college costs.

Family debt (with the exception of Investment Debt) isn't considered in the formula.

> *Example:* Family A and Family B have the same number of people, income, assets, and expenses, except Family A has just replaced their car which resulted in a monthly car payment (a debt). From Family A's viewpoint, they have less money for college than Family B. They think they should receive more aid. Family B believes Family A could have avoided the loan debt by repairing their car. Federal rules will treat both families the same.

The significance is not which family you might side with, but to learn that debt (your credit cards, loans, etc.) isn't considered.

The focus isn't to evaluate the law as fair or unfair, but to learn how to modify your portfolio and assets to receive more aid. Usually, debt will not help you obtain more aid.

There may be instances throughout this book where the law leaves you questioning the logic or feeling a sense of unfairness.

> *Example:* Two students earned money through part-time employment. The first student spent all her earnings on clothes, while the second student saved hers in a bank. All other factors were exactly the same. The first student will be eligible for more aid. The second student will be expected to use some of her assets, her discretionary earnings, to contribute toward paying college costs.

In this example, the first student, the spender is rewarded. The second student, the saver might see this as an unfair "Saver's Penalty."

Techniques (such as an IRA) can be used to shield the second student's assets from inclusion in the expected contribution, and thus, both students will qualify for an equal amount of aid.

Learning the law will help you make better choices.

Using the Law to Shift Assets

The law is far from perfect. The law penalizes those who save, especially when they save in the wrong place.

When two families have the same income and number of family members, there's no argument that based on income alone, they have the same need. Assuming there are no unusual circumstances (medical expenses, fire, flood, etc.) the difference in need will be a result of their spending habits. If all things are equal, when one family saves and the other spends, the spender family receives more aid. The spender has no assets, so is viewed to have the greater need. The spender is rewarded; the saver is penalized.

The common explanation for this dilemma is the government couldn't possibly track spending habits, so the law is as fair as it can be. Not everyone agrees. There are proposals to change the law so as to not require asset reporting, but today, you will have to plan for the law as written.

Suppose both families saved, but one used a savings account in the parents' name and the other saved in the student's name. The family who saved in the parents' name will receive more aid because parents' assets are weighted less in the formula. In this case, one family is penalized for ignorance, for simply saving in the wrong family member's name.

This book seeks to educate and show how to take advantage of the current law to qualify for additional aid.

Each year aid passes to families that might appear to be well-off. Students ask why the neighbors, with the home business, three cars, and boat, are receiving more aid. Most likely, that family is a spender, but also, that family probably knows the law.

The good news is you can do this too. You can take advantage of the law and take actions to change your current situation.

Selecting the right place to protect your assets is something every person has the right to do, and it isn't something only the wealthy are doing. Families of many different income levels are finding ways to increase their eligibility for aid.

The end result is the same: each person who applies these techniques will receive more aid than if they had not applied them. Everyone has equal opportunity to use the same rules.

FAFSA

FAFSA Overview

The Free Application for Federal Student Aid (FAFSA) is used to determine a student's need for aid. The first word in FAFSA is *Free*. There is no fee to apply. Take care when browsing the Internet to avoid sites that charge a fee. Go directly to http://www.FAFSA.ed.gov to file for free.

FAFSA Submission

The FAFSA must be submitted on a yearly basis. Using the online electronic submission is highly recommended. It's still a good idea to print out the form and read through it, to gain a general understanding prior to using the online application.

Submitting online:

- ✓ Is faster,
- ✓ Results in fewer mistakes,
- ✓ Allows the applicant to list ten schools (instead of four),
- ✓ Offers the option of pulling tax information directly from the IRS using the IRS Data Retrieval process,
- ✓ May allow the student to use the renewal system each year to provide updates
- ✓ Uses "Skip Logic" which allows the applicant to skip over some questions based on previous answers

Parents and students will each have a Personal Identification Number (PIN) obtained on submission or ahead of time from http://www.pin.ed.gov. Parents who want to keep their income private, should have control of both these PINs.

Attention to detail is critical when filling out the FAFSA. Every answer should be completed. If the answer is zero, do not leave it blank, but enter zero. Watch for questions asking for things like taxes paid, where you should use your tax return, not the figure on your Form W-2. Ask questions if you are unsure of an answer because the difference could result in more money in your pocket. Lastly, remember to sign the form, either with a pen (if you chose to use the paper form) or electronically.

FAFSA and EFC Resources

1. **New Links:** http://www.kidsandmoneytoday.com/fafsa-education/

2. **Student Aid Advice:** at http://studentaid.ed.gov

3. **FAFSA official site:** to complete your application go to http://www.fafsa.ed.gov

4. **Printable FAFSA (PDF):** a printable 2014-15 form at https://fafsa.ed.gov/fotw1415/pdf/PdfFafsa14-15.pdf (Prior to applying online, print and read this form to have a general idea of questions asked. Run an Internet search in January for the current year form.)

5. **FAFSA Demo:** at http://FAFSAdemo.test.ed.gov using user name: eddemo and password: FAFSAtest. (If demo is in the URL, you are in the demo test.)

6. **FAFSA Forecaster:** Estimate your eligibility use the FAFSA4caster at http://www.FAFSA4caster.ed.gov

7. **EFC Calculator/Estimator** can be found at https://bigfuture.collegeboard.org/pay-for-college/paying-your-share/expected-family-contribution-calculator

8. **Expected Family Contribution (EFC)** explanations (in depth) at http://ifap.ed.gov/efcformulaguide/attachments/091913EFCFormulaGuide1415.pdf

9. **Federal Student Aid Handbooks, Application and Verification Guides,** volumes, etc. at https://ifap.ed.gov/ifap/byAwardYear.jsp?type=fsahandbook
   * Volume 1, Student Eligibility
   * Volume 2, School Eligibility and Operations
   * Volume 3, Calculating Awards & Packaging
   * Volume 4, Processing Aid & Managing FSA Funds
   * Volume 5, Withdrawals and the Return of Title IV Funds
   * Volume 6, The Campus-Based Programs

FAFSA and EFC internet addresses often display the year. For example, the URL for No. 3. FAFSA Form (PDF) above shows 1415 which stands for academic year 2014-2015. This is an easy way to be sure you have the correct year's information.

FAFSA Deadlines

The FAFSA deadlines change each year. Students usually begin applying during the January prior to planned attendance. The deadline varies, with some schools falling as late as June 30th. Applicants can check with their school, online, or the front page of the printed FAFSA form for deadlines.

In most cases, students should apply as early as possible as some funds are released on a first-come first-serve basis.

The FAFSA acts as a "snapshot" of family finances. It's as if you took a financial picture on the date the application was signed.

If there is an upcoming financial event, relocation, change in marital status, a new dependent, etc., it might be beneficial to wait to file the FAFSA.

Also consider when to liquidate an asset. If liquidation changes an assets status from excluded to included and it's done before signing the FAFSA, the asset must now be reported and will affect your financial aid. (Assets are addressed throughout this book.)

FAFSA Corrections

Only some corrections can be made to the FAFSA after submission. The deadline for corrections falls in September and is posted on the FAFSA website.

> *Example*: FAFSA figures are checked to match those filed on your tax form. When the FAFSA is submitted prior to filing tax returns, estimated figures are used, and once the final figures are known, a correction is both needed and permitted.

EFC Overview

Your completed FAFSA is sent to the processing center, which computes your Expected Family Contribution (EFC). Your EFC is the amount your family is expected to pay toward college expenses. The figure comes from both the parents' and the student's income and assets.

Each school determines how much it will cost for the student to attend. This figure is called the Cost of Attendance (COA) and includes all the student's educational expenses for a period of enrollment (room and board, tuition, fees, travel costs, books, and any other expenses the school thinks the student must have). This figure is different for each school.

When you know your EFC and the COA, you can determine your family's financial need. Your financial need is the difference between the school cost and how much your family is expected to pay. (Keep in mind that you may not agree with your EFC.)

> Cost of Attendance (COA)
> − Expected Family Contribution (EFC)
> Student Financial Need

When the student is accepted at a school, the school will aim to fulfill the student's financial need. This is done by offering student aid (a mixture of scholarships, grants, loans, and work-study).

The goal of this book is to help your family receive more aid. To do this, you identify the components used to compute your EFC to see if they can be shifted in any way that would result in a lower EFC. The lower your Expected Family Contribution, the greater your aid offer will be.

In most cases, the EFC is calculated using a Regular Worksheet impacted by income, assets, the household size, and the number of students in college, but there are also two exceptions, and thus, there are actually **three possible ways to arrive at an EFC**:

1. The Automatic Zero EFC,

2. The Simplified Needs Test (SNT), and

3. The Regular EFC Worksheet.

The Automatic Zero EFC is not a calculation at all. If you meet certain criteria, you are automatically given an EFC of zero, meaning your family is not expected to contribute anything toward college. This would result in the greatest financial aid offer.

The Simplified Needs Test allows a family to exclude all *assets* when calculating the EFC. This is the next best category if you cannot qualify for the Automatic Zero EFC.

If you cannot meet the criteria for these two special categories, you use the Regular EFC Worksheet where your income, assets, household size, and students in college are used to calculate EFC. The criteria and calculations for these will be discussed in detail.

Terms Defined

Aid Terms

Award Year: The year the aid will be used

Base Year: Each calendar year prior to the student's college attendance. For students attending college from 2014 to 2015, the base year is 2013. Students graduating in four years will have four base years.

Cost of Attendance (COA): The cost of the student's educational expenses for a period of enrollment (room and board, tuition, fees, travel costs, books, etc.) as determined by each college. The best resource for this figure is to call each college, because even their own web pages may be out-of-date.

Expected Family Contribution (EFC): The amount a family is expected to contribute toward a student's college cost.

Financial Need: The basis on which colleges award *need-based* financial aid; the COA less your EFC.

Gap or Unmet Need: The difference between aid offered by the school and your financial need.

People

Student: The person (who may be married or single or may have children) who is applying for aid.

Noncustodial Parent: The applicant's legal parent, living in a separate household, who is not listed on the Free Application for Federal Student Aid (FAFSA).

Parents: The applicant's parent(s) required to be listed on the FAFSA. The term parents used in this book may refer to only one parent in cases of separation, divorce, or death. (*See also:* Who is a Parent)

Dislocated Worker: generally a person out of work or soon-to-be out of work. Six categories are defined in the Application and Verification Guide, at http://ifap. ed.gov/fsahandbook/attachments/1314AVGCh2.pdf

School References

Safe School: a school the student is sure to get in and can afford to attend with little or no financial aid; often an instate school so there is state aid and perhaps the student can live at home (to save on room and board).

Reach School: a school that might be questionable for attendance. It could be unaffordable or out of reach for merit reasons (grades, SAT scores, etc.).

Choice School: the student's or parents' first (or second) choice school. It may be a safe or a reach school.

Who is a Parent?

Beginning with the 2014-2015 FAFSA, dependent students must report the income and other information about both of the student's legal parents (biological or adoptive) if the parents are living together, regardless of the parents' marital status or gender. (*See also* p. 30). Complex issues arise when reporting income for common-law marriages, same-sex marriages, adoptions, stepparents, legal guardians, foster parents, students living with relatives, emancipated minors, orphans, homeless youths, student parents, and so forth. This book establishes a basic foundation for handling income and assets which should help in these complex situations.

Who is an Eligible Student?

Applicants wondering if they are eligible students should find out by completing the Free Application for Federal and Student Aid (FAFSA). Students should never assume they are ineligible for aid. Even if the family has high income or many assets, the form should still be completed. Even non U.S. citizens, such as green card holders can be eligible.[3] The same is true if a student has ever been convicted. Eligibility is based on income, assets, citizenship, education level, Selective Service registration, and other criteria, so applying is the best way to determine eligibility.

The FAFSA is also used to determine state and school aid. The student, who does not qualify for federal aid, still might qualify for an alternative form of aid, so this is another reason to apply.

---

3. Immihelp.com, *Benefits of a Green Card,* http://www.immihelp.com/ greencard/benefits-of-permanent-resident-card.html

Who is an Independent Student?

While this book uses the dependent student to explain concepts for financial aid computation, the following is a direct excerpt defining an Independent Student, provided for your convenience:

> "For the 2014–2015 Award Year, a student is automatically determined to be *independent* for *federal student aid* if he or she meets one or more of the following criteria:

* The student was born before January 1, 1991.
* The student is married or separated (but not divorced) as of the date of the application.
* At the beginning of the 2014–2015 school year, the student will be enrolled in a master's or doctoral degree program (such as MA, MBA, MD, JD, PhD, EdD, or graduate certificate, etc.).
* The student is currently serving on active duty in the U.S. Armed Forces or is a National Guard or Reserves enlistee called into federal active duty for purposes other than training.
* The student is a veteran of the U.S. Armed Forces.

[Veteran: A student who: (1) has engaged in active service in the U.S. Armed Forces (Army, Navy, Air Force, Marines, or Coast Guard), or has been a member of the National Guard or Reserves who was called to active duty for purposes other than training, or was a cadet or midshipman at one of the service academies, or attended a U.S. military academy preparatory school, and (2) was released under a condition other than dishonorable. A veteran is also a student who does not meet this definition now but will by June 30, 2015.]

* The student has or will have one or more children who receive more than half of their support from him or her between July 1, 2014 and June 30, 2015.
* The student has dependent(s) (other than children or spouse) who live with him or her and who receive more than half of their support from the student, now and through June 30, 2015.

* At *any time* since the student turned age 13, both of the student's parents were deceased, the student was in foster care, or a dependent or ward of the court.

* As determined by a court in the student's state of legal residence, the student is now or was upon reaching the age of majority, an emancipated minor (released from control by his or her parent or guardian).

* As determined by a court in the student's state of legal residence, the student is now or was upon reaching the age of majority, in legal guardianship.

* On or after July 1, 2013, the student was determined by a high school or school district homeless liaison to be an unaccompanied youth who was homeless or was self-supporting and at risk of being homeless.

* On or after July 1, 2013, the student was determined by the director of an emergency shelter or transitional housing program funded by the U.S. Department of Housing and Urban Development to be an unaccompanied youth who was homeless or was self-supporting and at risk of being homeless.

* At any time on or after July 1, 2013, the student was determined by a director of a runaway or homeless youth basic center or transitional living program to be an unaccompanied youth who was homeless or was self-supporting and at risk of being homeless.

* The student was determined by the college financial aid administrator to be an unaccompanied youth who is homeless or is self-supporting and at risk of being homeless.

For students who do not meet any of the above criteria but who have documented unusual circumstances, an FAA can override their dependency status from dependent to independent. For information about dependency overrides, see the Application and Verification Guide, which is part of the Federal Student Aid Handbook and can be found on the IFAP Web site."[4]

---

4. 2014-2015 EFC Formula Guide, *What is the definition of an independent student,* p. 3, http://ifap.ed.gov/efcformulaguide/attachments/091913EFCFormulaGuide1415.pdf

Unusual and Special Circumstances

The FAFSA must always be completed by the deadline to receive aid. All questions must be answered to the extent possible. It is important to obtain personal guidance from counselors, Financial Aid Advisors at the college, or the FAFSA hotline for any special circumstances because a mistake on the FAFSA can result in the loss of several thousands of dollars in aid.

This book uses a typical dependent child to explain calculations. Unusual circumstances are not covered, but the general overview of the factors that affect aid will still allow you to plan a financial strategy, and might shed light on ideas to research further. (*See also*, Professional Judgment p. 144.)

The list below is provided as a quick reference of some common unusual circumstances to see if any might apply to you:

* Students attending less than nine months
* Students convicted of federal or state offenses
* Incarceration
* Issues surrounding students with dependents, who currently live with the student's parents
* Take-back mortgages
* Assets with liens, jointly owned, or contested ownership
* Loss of employment
* Dislocated worker issues
* Special students: foster children, orphans, homeless, etc.
* Unusually high medical expenses
* Veteran's issues
* Same-sex unions (Note: "...beginning with the 2014-2015 federal student aid form, the Department will—for the first time—collect income and other information from a dependent student's legal parents regardless of the parents' marital status or gender, if those parents live together..[5])

---

5. *Education Department Announces Changes to FAFSA Form to More Accurately and Fairly Assess Students' Need for Aid* http://www.ed.gov/news/press-releases/education-department-announces-changes-fafsa-form-more-accurately-and-fairly-ass

Expected Family Contribution

The information collected on the FAFSA form is used to compute the Expected Family Contribution (EFC). The EFC is the amount a family can be expected to contribute toward college expenses.

The EFC is the sum of

1. The **parents'** expected contribution, plus

2. The **student's** expected contribution from Available Income (AI), plus

3. The **student's** expected contribution from assets.

Example: Regular EFC Worksheet, Dependent Student

EXPECTED FAMILY CONTRIBUTION	
PARENTS' CONTRIBUTION (from line 28)	
STUDENT'S CONTRIBUTION FROM AI (from line 44) +	
STUDENT'S CONTRIBUTION FROM ASSETS (from line 50) +	
51. EXPECTED FAMILY CONTRIBUTION (standard contribution for nine-month enrollment)** If negative, enter zero. =	

The family EFC is subtracted from the Cost of Attendance (COA) to determine the student's financial need:

> Cost of Attendance (COA)
> − Expected Family Contribution (EFC)
> Student Financial Need

With a greater understanding of the components of EFC, you can take steps to reduce it and thereby maximize the financial aid received. Some students will qualify for an Automatic Zero EFC or qualify to use a Simplified Worksheet. This depends on:

1. The type of tax return filed,

2. Whether a means-tested federal benefit was received,

3. If the parent is a dislocated worker, and

4. The parents' taxable income (defined as AGI for tax filers or combined income earned from work for non-filers)

Automatic Zero EFC

The best scenario would be to have an Automatic Zero EFC, which means neither the parents, nor the student, is expected to contribute toward expenses. The eligibility rules are provided next as direct quotes. For these rules, your income is the Adjusted Gross Income (AGI) on your tax return or for non-tax filers, the income on your W-2 form (plus any other earnings from work not included on the W-2s). If you file the 1040 only to receive education credits, you *are eligible* for the lower tax forms.

Dependent Student - Automatic Zero EFC

The 2014-2015 rules are:

"For the 2014–2015 Award Year, a dependent student automatically qualifies for a zero EFC if both (1) and (2) are true.

(1) Anyone included in the parents' household size (as defined on the FAFSA) received benefits during 2012 or 2013 from any of the designated means-tested federal benefit programs: the SSI Program, SNAP, the Free and Reduced Price School Lunch Program, the TANF Program, and WIC; OR

The student's parents:

* filed or were eligible to file a 2013 IRS Form 1040A or 1040EZ,
* filed a 2013 IRS Form 1040 but were not required to do so, or
* were not required to file any income tax return; OR
* the student's parent is a dislocated worker.

AND

(2) The 2013 income of the student's parents is $24,000 or less."[6]

---

6. EFC Formula Guide 2014-2015, *Which students qualify for an Automatic Zero EFC calculation?*, p. 5-6, http://ifap.ed.gov/efcformulaguide/attachments/091913EFCFormulaGuide1415.pdf

Independent Student - Automatic Zero EFC

"An independent student **with dependents other than a spouse** automatically qualifies for a zero EFC if both (1) below and (2) on the next page are true:

(1) Anyone included in the **student's** household size (as defined on the FAFSA) received benefits during 2012 or 2013 from any of the designated means-tested federal benefit programs: the SSI Program, SNAP, the Free and Reduced Price School Lunch Program, the TANF Program, and WIC; **OR**

the **student and student's spouse** (if the student is married) both

* filed or were eligible to file a 2013 IRS Form 1040A or 1040EZ,
* filed a 2013 IRS Form 1040 but were not required to do so, or
* were not required to file any income tax return; **OR**

the **student** (or the student's spouse, if any) is a dislocated worker.

AND

(2) The **student's** (and spouse's) 2013 income is $24,000 or less.

Note: An independent student without dependents other than a spouse is not eligible for an automatic zero EFC."[7]

Also note: Per the FAFSA instructions, if you file the 1040 only to receive education credits, you should answer "yes" on the FAFSA concerning eligibility for lower forms.

Independent Student with Only a Spouse Dependent

There is no Automatic Zero for an independent student whose only dependent is a spouse.

---

7. Ibid, p. 6-7

Iraq and Afghanistan Service Grant & Automatic Zero

Students with a parent or guardian who died as a result of service in Iraq or Afghanistan may fall under special EFC rules.

> "Schools will consider the EFC to be zero for Pell-eligible students with a parent or guardian who was a member of the U.S. Armed Forces and who died as a result of service in Iraq or Afghanistan after September 11, 2001.
>
> These students must have been less than 24 years old or enrolled in college when the parent or guardian died."[8]

Students who think they might qualify should consult their guidance counselor and financial aid officer at the college. Their EFC will be calculated by the processing center, but the school should use a zero when creating aid packets.

For students, who *are not* Pell-eligible:

> "Students in this situation who are not Pell-eligible because their EFC is too high will be able to receive an Iraq and Afghanistan service grant (see Volume 1, Chapter 6 [of the Application and Verification Guide]) in the same amount of the Pell grant they would have been eligible for with a zero EFC. However, for these students the school uses the EFC calculated by the CPS for packaging instead of zero."[9]

In essence, Pell-eligible students get their EFC reduced to zero and thus can receive the maximum Pell Grant, where as those who are not Pell-eligible can receive the Iraq and Afghanistan Service Grant in the same amount as the Pell grant, as if they had a zero EFC.

---

8. Application and Verification Guide 2013-2014, *Expected Family Contribution (EFC)*, "DoD Match and Iraq and Afghanistan Service Grant," p. 37, http://ifap.ed.gov/fsahandbook/attachments/1314AVGCh3.pdf

9. Ibid.

EFC Formula

When students are ineligible for an Automatic Zero, the processing center use one of three categories to calculate the EFC. Each category has both a Simplified and a Regular Worksheet:

1. Dependent Student, Worksheet A (Simplified or Regular)

2. Independent Student, Worksheet B (Simplified or Regular)

3. Independent Students with Dependents Other Than Spouse, Worksheet C (Simplified or Regular)

If you can't qualify for the Automatic Zero EFC, the next best thing is to be able to use a Simplified Worksheet.

Simplified EFC Formula - Simplified Needs Test (SNT)

The Simplified EFC Worksheets disregard assets. They appear as blackened out blocks (making the form simpler) as shown below.

EXPECTED FAMILY CONTRIBUTION	
PARENTS' CONTRIBUTION (from line 28)	
STUDENT'S CONTRIBUTION FROM AI (from line 44) +	
STUDENT'S CONTRIBUTION FROM ASSETS (from line 50) +	
51. EXPECTED FAMILY CONTRIBUTION standard contribution for nine month enrollment. If negative, enter zero.** =	

You still provide your asset information on the FAFSA, and the result is the processing center creates two EFCs:

1. A primary EFC which excludes assets and

2. A secondary EFC including assets:[10]

If you qualify to use a Simplified Worksheet, you will not have to worry about shielding your assets for federal aid, but despite this federal exclusion, sometimes your assets will still be included for your state or school aid.

---

10. Application and Verification Guide 2013-2014, *Expected Family Contribution*, "Simplified Formula," p. 35-36, http://ifap.ed.gov/fsahandbook/attachments/1314AVGCh3.pdf

Dependent Student - Simplified EFC

The eligibility rules for the Simplified Worksheets are provided next as direct quotes from the 2014-2015 EFC Formula Guide. For the Simplified Needs Test, income is your Adjusted Gross Income (AGI) on your tax return or for non-tax filers, the income on your W-2 form (plus any other earnings from work not included on the W-2s).

"For the 2014–2015 Award Year, a **dependent** student qualifies for the simplified EFC formula if both (1) below and (2) on the next page are true:

(1) [One of the following]

* Anyone included in the **parents'** household size (as defined on the FAFSA) received benefits during 2012 or 2013 from any of the designated means-tested federal benefit programs: the Supplemental Security Income (SSI) Program, the Supplemental Nutrition Assistance Program (SNAP), the Free and Reduced Price School Lunch Program, the Temporary Assistance for Needy Families (TANF) Program, and the Special Supplemental Nutrition Program for Women, Infants, and Children (WIC); **OR**

* the student's **parents**: filed or were eligible to file a 2013 IRS Form 1040A or 1040EZ, filed a 2013 IRS Form 1040 but were not required to do so, or were not required to file any income tax return; **OR**

* the student's **parent** is a dislocated worker.

AND

(2) The 2013 income of the student's **parents is $49,999** or less."[11]

---

11. EFC Formula Guide 2014-2015, *Which students qualify for the Simplified EFC formulas?*, p. 4-5, http://ifap.ed.gov/efcformulaguide/attachments/09191 3EFCFormulaGuide1415.pdf

Independent Student - Simplified EFC

"For the 2014–2015 Award Year, an **independent** student qualifies for the simplified EFC formula if both (1) and (2) below are true:

(1) [One of the following]

* Anyone included in the **student's** household size (as defined on the FAFSA) received benefits during 2012 or 2013 from any of the designated means-tested federal benefit programs: the SSI Program, SNAP, the Free and Reduced Price School Lunch Program, the TANF Program, and WIC; **OR**

* the student and **student's** spouse (if the student is married) **both**

    * filed or were eligible to file a 2013 IRS Form 1040A or 1040EZ,

    * filed a 2013 IRS Form 1040 but were not required to do so, **OR**

    * were not required to file any income tax return; **OR**

* the student (or the student's spouse, if any) is a dislocated worker.

AND

(2) The **student's (and spouse's)** 2013 income is $49,999 or less."[12]

Note: Per the FAFSA instructions, if you file the 1040 only to receive education credits, you should answer "yes" on the FAFSA concerning eligibility for lower forms.

Dependent Student - Regular EFC

Students who do not qualify for either the Automatic Zero EFC or for the Simplified Needs Test will use the Regular Worksheet.

---

12. Ibid., p. 5.

For understanding basic concepts, the **Dependent Student, Regular Worksheet (as shown) is used in this book.** Students eligible to use the Independent Student Regular Worksheets will follow the same general rules, with parents' items omitted.

The first page of the Regular worksheet contains the parents' information and the second page contains the student's.

Dependent Student, Regular Worksheet - Parent Information (p. 1)

2014–2015 EFC FORMULA A : DEPENDENT STUDENT

REGULAR WORKSHEET Page 1 — A

PARENTS' INCOME IN 2013

1. Parents' Adjusted Gross Income (FAFSA/SAR #85)
   If negative, enter zero.

2. a. Parent 1 (father/mother/stepparent) income earned from work (FAFSA/SAR #88)
   b. Parent 2 (father/mother/stepparent) income earned from work (FAFSA/SAR #89) +

   Total parents' income earned from work =

3. Parents' Taxable Income
   (If tax filers, enter the amount from line 1 above. If non-tax filers, enter the amount from line 2.)*

4. Total untaxed income and benefits:
   (Total of FAFSA/SAR #94a. through 94i.) +

5. Taxable and untaxed income
   (sum of line 3 and line 4) =

6. Total additional financial information
   (Total of FAFSA/SAR #93a. through 93f.) −

7. **TOTAL INCOME**
   (line 5 minus line 6) May be a negative number. =

ALLOWANCES AGAINST PARENTS' INCOME

8. 2013 U.S. income tax paid (FAFSA/SAR #86)
   (tax filers only) If negative, enter zero.

9. State and other tax allowance
   (Table A1) If negative, enter zero. +

10. Parent 1 (father/mother/stepparent) Social Security tax allowance (Table A2) +

11. Parent 2 (father/mother/stepparent) Social Security tax allowance (Table A2) +

12. Income protection allowance (Table A3) +

13. Employment expense allowance:
   - Two working parents (Parents' Marital Status is "married" or "unmarried and both parents living together"): 35% of the lesser of the earned incomes, or $4,000, whichever is less
   - One-parent families: 35% of earned income, or $4,000, whichever is less
   - Two-parent families, one working parent: enter zero +

14. **TOTAL ALLOWANCES** =

*STOP HERE if the following are true:

Line 3 is $24,000 or less **and**

- The parents are eligible to file a 2013 IRS Form 1040A or 1040EZ (they are not required to file a 2013 Form 1040) or they are not required to file any income tax return **or**
- Anyone included in the parents' household size (as defined on the FAFSA) received benefits during 2012 or 2013 from any of the designated means-tested federal benefit programs **or**
- Either of the parents is a dislocated worker.

If these circumstances are true, the Expected Family Contribution is automatically zero.

AVAILABLE INCOME

Total income (from line 7)

Total allowances (from line 14) −

15. **AVAILABLE INCOME (AI)**
   May be a negative number. =

PARENTS' CONTRIBUTION FROM ASSETS

16. Cash, savings & checking (FAFSA/SAR #90)

17. Net worth of investments**
   (FAFSA/SAR #91)
   If negative, enter zero.

18. Net worth of business and/or investment farm
   (FAFSA/SAR #92)
   If negative, enter zero.

19. Adjusted net worth of business/farm
   (Calculate using Table A4.) +

20. **Net worth** (sum of lines 16, 17, and 19) =

21. Education savings and asset protection allowance (Table A5) −

22. Discretionary net worth
   (line 20 minus line 21) =

23. Asset conversion rate × .12

24. **CONTRIBUTION FROM ASSETS**
   If negative, enter zero. =

PARENTS' CONTRIBUTION

AVAILABLE INCOME (AI) (from line 15)

CONTRIBUTION FROM ASSETS (from line 24) +

25. **Adjusted Available Income (AAI)**
   May be a negative number. =

26. **Total parents' contribution from AAI**
   (Calculate using Table A6.) If negative, enter zero.

27. **Number in college in 2014–2015**
   (Exclude parents) (FAFSA/SAR #74) +

28. **PARENTS' CONTRIBUTION** (standard contribution for nine-month enrollment)***
   If negative, enter zero. =

**Do *not* include the fami[...]

***To calculate the parents[...] enrollment, see page 11[...]

① (line 28)
Parent Contribution

(Individual blocks are shown larger when discussed later.)

The individual blocks consolidate information collected from the FAFSA. This information is used to arrive at the family EFC. Understanding the components of each block will bring to light items that you might adjust to result in increased aid. The blocks from the form are illustrated as a flow chart on the next page.

Dependent Student, Regular Worksheet - Student Information (p. 2)

REGULAR WORKSHEET Page 2 **A**		

STUDENT'S INCOME IN 2013	
29. Adjusted Gross Income (FAFSA/SAR #36) If negative, enter zero.	
30. Income earned from work (FAFSA/SAR #39)	
31. Taxable Income (If tax filer, enter the amount from line 29 above. If non-tax filer, enter the amount from line 30.)	
32. Total untaxed income and benefits (Total of FAFSA/SAR #45a. through 45j.) +	
33. Taxable and untaxed income (sum of line 31 and line 32) =	
34. Total additional financial information (Total of FAFSA/SAR #44a. through 44f.) ‑	
35. **TOTAL INCOME** (line 33 minus line 34) = May be a negative number.	

STUDENT'S CONTRIBUTION FROM ASSETS		
45. Cash, savings & checking (FAFSA/SAR #41)		
46. Net worth of investments* (FAFSA/SAR #42) If negative, enter zero.		
47. Net worth of business and/or investment farm (FAFSA/SAR #43) If negative, enter zero. +		
48. Net worth (sum of lines 45 through 47) =		
49. Assessment rate ×	.20	
50. STUDENT'S CONTRIBUTION FROM ASSETS =		

EXPECTED FAMILY CONTRIBUTION		
PARENTS' CONTRIBUTION (from line 28)		①
STUDENT'S CONTRIBUTION FROM AI (from line 44) +		②
STUDENT'S CONTRIBUTION FROM ASSETS (from line 50) +		③
51. **EXPECTED FAMILY CONTRIBUTION** (standard contribution for nine-month enrollment)** If negative, enter zero. =		④

ALLOWANCES AGAINST STUDENT INCOME		
36. 2013 U.S. income tax paid (FAFSA/SAR #37) (tax filers only) If negative, enter zero.		
37. State and other tax allowance (Table A7) If negative, enter zero. +		
38. Social Security tax allowance (Table A2) +		
39. Income protection allowance +	6,260
40. Allowance for parents' negative Adjusted Available Income (If line 25 is negative, enter line 25 as a positive number in line 40. If line 25 is zero or positive, enter zero in line 40.) +		
41. TOTAL ALLOWANCES =		

③ (line 50)
Student Contribution From Assets

(line 51)
The Family EFC
①+②+③=④

STUDENT'S CONTRIBUTION FROM INCOME	
Total income (from line 35)	
Total allowances (from line 41) −	
42. **Available income (AI)** =	
43. Assessment of AI ×	.50
44. STUDENT'S CONTRIBUTION FROM AI = If negative, enter zero.	

② (line 44)
Student Available Income (AI) Contribution

(Individual blocks are shown larger when discussed later.)

Calculating the EFC

To begin understanding how the EFC is calculated, we will explain each block from the Dependent Student, Regular Worksheet and also use the EFC Flow Chart shown below.

The EFC Flow Chart simplifies the two forms; summarizing EFC Calculation.

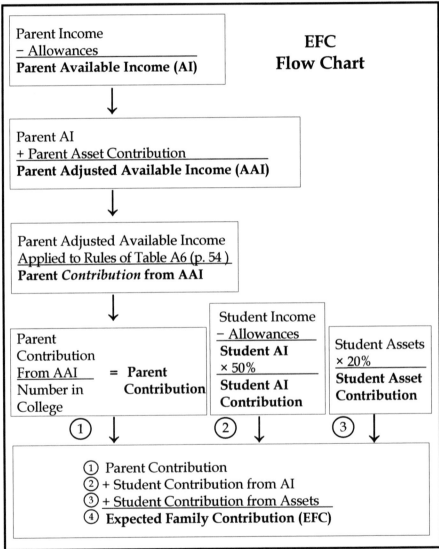

To begin understanding calculations, look at the final block on the form. The EFC is the sum of three calculations:

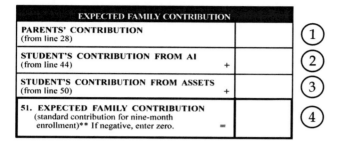

As previously mentioned, these calculations come from three components:

I.   Available Income (AI),

II. Contribution from assets, and

III. The number of children in college.

If you focus on how these three components are defined by law and how they are used in the calculations, you can find ways to manipulate them to reduce your overall EFC. Available Income (AI) is explained first.

I. Available Income (AI) for the EFC

Available Income for EFC is the total income (including untaxed income and benefits) less certain allowances, as shown on both the flow chart and EFC form:

Parent Income	Student Income
− Allowances	− Allowances
Parent Available Income (AI)	**Student AI**

Example: Parent AI, Dependent Student, Regular EFC Worksheet

AVAILABLE INCOME		
Total income (from line 7)		
Total allowances (from line 14)	−	
15. AVAILABLE INCOME (AI) May be a negative number.	=	

Components of Parent and Student Total Income

All income must be reported from work and other sources, even if a tax return was not filed. The processing center pulls these figures from your FAFSA and uses the EFC worksheet to compute your EFC.

The FAFSA application is completed using base year income:

> **The Base Year:** is the year prior to the student's college attendance. For example, parents will use their 2013 tax forms to declare income for a student attending college from 2014-2015.

The areas you might influence to impact your income figure are:

1. **Taxable Income:** Defined by IRS laws (lines 7 through 21 on a Form 1040); the goal is to reduce these

2. **Income Exclusions:** Items not counted as income

3. **Untaxed Income and Benefits:** Items *added* to income, even if they do not appear on a tax return

4. **Taxable Income Offsets:** Amounts reported on the FAFSA but *excluded* from income

The more you can increase income exclusions and offsets, and decrease untaxed income and benefits, the lower your EFC will be, and the result will be more financial aid.

The rules categorizing types of income are the same for both parents and students.

Student Taxable Income

Employed students report their taxable income. These funds are considered to be available for college, regardless as to whether they were saved or spent.

Depending on how earnings are saved, they may be assessed as an asset. Working students should consider saving paychecks in a Roth IRA (instead of a savings account) so what is income this year will not turn into an asset next year (*See* IRAs, p. 72).

There are mixed viewpoints as to how many hours a student should actually work and for what annual salary, as working may impact grades and graduation. (*See* Employed Students, p. 46).

Excerpts from the Dependent Student, Regular EFC Worksheet

Parents' Income

PARENTS' INCOME IN 2013		
1. Parents' Adjusted Gross Income (FAFSA/SAR #85) If negative, enter zero.		
2. a. Parent 1 (father/mother/stepparent) income earned from work (FAFSA/SAR #88)		
2. b. Parent 2 (father/mother/stepparent) income earned from work (FAFSA/SAR #89) +		
Total parents' income earned from work =		
3. Parents' Taxable Income (If tax filers, enter the amount from line 1 above. If non-tax filers, enter the amount from line 2.)*		
4. Total untaxed income and benefits: (Total of FAFSA/SAR #94a. through 94i.) +		←**Untaxed Income and Benefits** (p. 33)
5. Taxable and untaxed income (sum of line 3 and line 4) =		
6. Total additional financial information (Total of FAFSA/SAR #93a. through 93f.) −		←**Also referred to as Income Offsets** (p. 35)
7. **TOTAL INCOME** (line 5 minus line 6) May be a negative number. =		

Student's Income

STUDENT'S INCOME IN 2013		
29. Adjusted Gross Income (FAFSA/SAR #36) If negative, enter zero.		
30. Income earned from work (FAFSA/SAR #39)		
31. Taxable Income (If tax filer, enter the amount from line 29 above. If non-tax filer, enter the amount from line 30.)		
32. Total untaxed income and benefits (Total of FAFSA/SAR #45a. through 45j.) +		←**Untaxed Income and Benefits** (p. 33)
33. Taxable and untaxed income (sum of line 31 and line 32) =		
34. Total additional financial information (Total of FAFSA/SAR #44a. through 44f.) −		←**Also referred to as Income Offsets** (p. 35)
35. **TOTAL INCOME** (line 33 minus line 34) = May be a negative number.		

Parent Taxable Income

Beginning with the 2014-2015 FAFSA, a dependent student will be required to include income and other information about both of the student's legal parents (biological or adoptive) **if the parents are living together,** regardless of the parents' marital status or gender. Unmarried parents living together and married same-sex couples are required to report both parents' income and assets.

In general, dependent students must list their parents' income, even if the parents decline to list the student as a qualifying child for the dependent exemption on their tax return, and even if the parents will not be contributing toward the student's education. (An exception exists for single, separated, or divorced parents.)

Single, Separated, or Divorced Parents

A change in marital status creates complexities but it also offers opportunities for increased aid. In the case of single or divorced parents (living separately), students list the income of the parent with whom they lived the longest during the previous 12 months.[13]

If a divorce is pending, both parents have income, and one will move out of the home, by waiting to submit the FAFSA until after the divorce is finalized, one parent's income will be eliminated from the calculations, and thus lower the EFC (resulting in more aid). Parents might also consider federal aid when deciding custody, especially if the child is already a teenager. Living with the parent with lower income usually results in more federal aid.

Marriage & Remarriage

Recall that the FAFSA is a "snapshot" of the family finances as of the date signed. The parent or student could get married in the base year, or in the award year but before signing the FAFSA, or in the award year but after signing the FAFSA. You probably won't move your marriage date for FAFSA results, but you might decide when to sign the FAFSA based on your upcoming marriage.

If the new spouse has income, this will increase the EFC, but the new spouse also increases your Household Count (*See* p. 43), which lowers the EFC. Additionally, if the new spouse is older,

---

13. U.S. Department of Education Federal Student Aid, *FAFSA Application,* 2014-2015, *Notes for Step 4,* p. 9, https://fafsa.ed.gov/fotw1415/pdf/PdfFafsa14-15.pdf

the Asset Protection Allowance (*See* p. 51) may factor in (causing a decrease in EFC). You might compute the EFC both ways (using figures prior to the marriage and figures in place after the marriage) and choose the better outcome.

Once the FAFSA is signed, it cannot be updated for a change in marital status. This makes sense because the FAFSA is a snapshot of one's financial situation and marital status as of that particular day.

> "Report your marital status as of the date you sign your FAFSA. If your marital status changes after you sign your FAFSA, check with the financial aid office at the college. Consistent with the Supreme Court decision holding Section 3 of the Defense of Marriage Act (DOMA) unconstitutional, **same-sex couples** must report their marital status as married if they were legally married in a state or other jurisdiction (foreign country) that permits same-sex marriage, without regard to where the couple resides"[14]

> However, "Only the opposite sex spouse of a legal parent is considered a *stepparent* for FAFSA purposes. However, if a **same-sex** partner has become a legal parent by adopting the dependent student, information from each legal parent would be collected."[15]

If the marriage date is before the FAFSA submission, even if the marriage is in the new calendar year, the new spouse's income and assets are reported and used in the EFC computation.

> *Stepparent Example:* A custodial parent (Mom), remarries and the new stepparent provides no financial support. Dad sends support every month. This student will report Mom's and the stepparent's income on the FAFSA.

If the new spouse's income is significant, you might consider delaying the marriage or remarriage until after signing the FAFSA, or perhaps, even until after the student has graduated college. This shields the new spouse's income and assets from counting in the EFC formula.

---

14. U.S. Department of Education Federal Student Aid, *FAFSA Application*, 2014-2015, p. 2, https://fafsa.ed.gov/fotw1415/pdf/PdfFafsa14-15.pdf

15. Attachment A to DCL GEN-13-12 Comparison of Parental Data Collected on FAFSA and Used in the EFC Calculation, https://fafsa.ed.gov/fotw1415/pdf/PdfFafsa14-15.pdf

Income Exclusions

Per the Application and Verification Guide, the following are good to have; not included in the EFC computation:

a. Student aid

b. Veterans' Education Benefits

c. The value of on-base housing

d. Rent subsidies for low-income housing

e. Payments and services received from states for foster care or adoption assistance

f. Per capita payments to Native Americans

g. Heating/fuel assistance

h. Flexible Spending Arrangements (accounts) (FSAs)

i. Welfare benefits, untaxed Social Security benefits, and the Earned Income Credit and the Additional Child Tax Credit

j. Combat pay, foreign income exclusion, and credit for federal tax on special fuels

k. In-kind support including but not limited to the following:

   * SNAP (formerly Food Stamp Program)
   * Women, Infants, and Children Program (WIC)
   * Food Distribution programs
   * National School Lunch and School Breakfast programs
   * Commodity Supplemental Food Program (CSFP)
   * Special Milk Program for children
   * Daycare provided by the Social Services Block Grant Program (if the recipient receives reimbursement for child care expenses, that amount is reported as income)
   * WIA (formerly JTPA) educational benefits
   * Rollover pensions
   * Payments and services received from states for foster care or adoption assistance, under Part A or Part E of Title IV of the Social Security Act

l. American Opportunity Act Credit: "[The refundable portion] does not appear on the lines of the FAFSA for the education tax credits, nor does it count as untaxed income."

Untaxed Income and Benefits (Added to Income)

The following are added to income and thus increase your EFC. You might want to try to reduce these to qualify for more aid.

a. "Payments to tax-deferred or sheltered pension and savings plans (paid directly or withheld from earnings). This includes untaxed portions of 401(k) and 403(b) plans. These types of payments are listed in boxes 12a through 12d of the W-2 and will have one of the following codes: D, E, F, G, H, or S. *Note* that employer contributions to these plans shouldn't be reported as an untaxed benefit

b. Deductible IRA or Keogh payments. Payments to an IRA or Keogh plan that are excluded from taxation are reported as untaxed income. These amounts appear on the tax return. and include SEP and SIMPLE contributions

  — *Note:* You might consider contributing the maximum amounts to retirement plans (options c and d) in base years if it would reduce your AGI to meet the threshold requirements for the Automatic Zero or Simplified Needs Test (SNT).

c. Child support received for all children.

d. Tax-exempt interest income. Certain types of interest, such as interest on municipal bonds, are tax-exempt. This amount is on line 8b on both the 1040 and 1040A forms.

e. Untaxed IRA distributions and pension or annuity payments. A tax filer determines how much of his IRA distribution or pension or annuity payment is taxable when he completes his tax return. The applicant reports the untaxed portion, which is determined from the tax return, but should not include rollovers(transfers of funds from one IRA to another).

f. Housing, food, and other living allowances. Include clergy, military basic allowance for subsistence, money received to pay for rent, free use of a house or apartment (the rent or market value of a comparable residence), the value of free room or board received for a job that was not awarded as student financial aid (including resident advisor positions that provide free room and board as part of the student's non-need-based employment compensation).

g. Veterans' noneducation benefits: disability, the death pension, Dependency and Indemnity Compensation (DIC), and Veterans Affairs (VA) educational work-study allowances.

h. Any other untaxed income not reported elsewhere. This can include disability (but *not Social Security disability*), worker's compensation, interest income on education IRAs, untaxed portions of Railroad Retirement benefits, black lung benefits, refugee assistance, the untaxed portion of capital gains, and foreign income that wasn't taxed by any government and isn't part of the Foreign Earned Income Exclusion.

EXCEPTIONS: Don't include student aid, Earned Income Credit, additional child tax credit, welfare payments, untaxed Social Security benefits, Supplemental Security Income, Workforce Investment Act educational benefits, on-base military housing or a military housing allowance, combat pay, benefits from Flexible Spending Arrangements (FSAs) (e.g. Cafeteria plans), foreign income exclusion or credit for federal tax on special fuels.

i. Money received. The student reports any cash support received. A dependent does not count parental support, with one exception: money from a noncustodial parent that is not part of a legal child support agreement is untaxed income to the student.

— Cash support includes money, allowance, gifts, loans, repayment of student loans, plus housing, food, clothing, car payments or expenses (auto insurance), medical and dental care, college costs, and money paid to someone else on his behalf.

* *Example:* Report the amount a friend or relative pays for a student's electric bill or rent.

— *Third-party Qualified Tuition Plans (QTPs):* The noncustodial parent's or relatives' distributions from QTPs are included as untaxed income or money received for the *student.*"[16]

---

16. Application and Verification Guide 2013-2014, Chapter 2, *Filling out the FAFSA,* http://ifap.ed.gov/fsahandbook/attachments/1314AVG.pdf

Additional Financial Information (Income Offsets)

Income Offsets are items that may appear on a tax return but are *excluded* from need analysis. They are subtracted to reduce EFC and thus, good to have:

a. Education tax credits (line 49 of the Form 1040)

b. Child Support payments made

c. Taxable earnings from need-based work programs including Federal Work-Study (FWS)

d. Taxable student grant and scholarship aid

e. Taxable combat pay included in Adjusted Gross Income

f. Earnings from work under a cooperative education program offered by a college.[17]

We've discussed the components of Parent and Student Income, the shaded items below. Allowances deducted are discussed next.

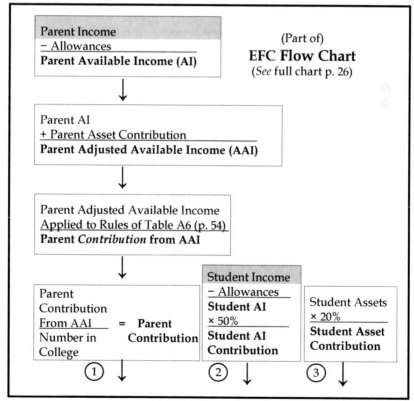

---

17. Ibid, p. 20.

Total Allowances (Reduce Income)

After arriving at Total Income, you subtract certain allowances to arrive at the Available Income (AI) used for computing the Expected Family Contribution. This concept is generally the same for students and parents.

Excerpts from the Regular EFC Worksheet, Dependent Student

AVAILABLE INCOME		
Total income (from line 7)		
Total allowances (from line 14)	−	
15. AVAILABLE INCOME (AI) May be a negative number.	=	

STUDENT'S CONTRIBUTION FROM INCOME		
Total income (from line 35)		
Total allowances (from line 41)	−	
42. Available income (AI)	=	

If you can *increase* your allowances, you will reduce Available Income (AI), and reduce your Expected Family Contribution.

The student allowances permitted include:

1. U.S. Income Tax Paid

2. Social Security Tax Allowance

3. State and Other Tax Allowances

4. Income Protection Allowance (varies for parents; uses a flat rate for students)

5. Employment Expense Allowance (only for parents)

6. Student allowance for parents' negative income

The government does not expect you to use all of your income for college expenses. These allowances try to make adjustments for the expenses every family encounters. For example, everyone spends money on taxes and everyone needs money for food, clothing, and shelter. Each allowance is discussed next.

Excerpts from the Dependent Student, Regular EFC Worksheet

Parent Allowances from the Dependent Student Worksheet

ALLOWANCES AGAINST PARENTS' INCOME	
8. 2013 U.S. income tax paid (FAFSA/SAR #86) (tax filers only) If negative, enter zero.	
9. State and other tax allowance (Table A1) If negative, enter zero. +	
10. Parent 1 (father/mother/stepparent) Social Security tax allowance (Table A2) +	
11. Parent 2 (father/mother/stepparent) Social Security tax allowance (Table A2) +	
12. Income protection allowance (Table A3) +	
13. Employment expense allowance: • Two working parents (Parents' Marital Status is "married" or "unmarried and both parents living together"): 35% of the lesser of the earned incomes, or $4,000, whichever is less • One-parent families: 35% of earned income, or $4,000, whichever is less • Two-parent families, one working parent: enter zero +	
14. TOTAL ALLOWANCES =	

Student Allowances from the Dependent Student Worksheet

ALLOWANCES AGAINST STUDENT INCOME	
36. 2013 U.S. income tax paid (FAFSA/SAR #37) (tax filers only) If negative, enter zero.	
37. State and other tax allowance (Table A7) If negative, enter zero. +	
38. Social Security tax allowance (Table A2) +	
39. Income protection allowance +	**6,260**
40. Allowance for parents' negative Adjusted Available Income (If line 25 is negative, enter line 25 as a positive number in line 40. If line 25 is zero or positive, enter zero in line 40.) +	
41. TOTAL ALLOWANCES =	

U.S. Income Tax Paid.

The U.S. Income Tax Paid comes from your filed tax form. A higher tax amount (paying more taxes) results in a lower EFC. If your tax form shows a negative number, the FAFSA entry is zero. If no tax return was filed, no allowance is permitted.

Since paying higher taxes lowers your EFC, you might plan your taxes for a period of years where the net result is the same amount of taxes paid, but higher taxes are paid in the *base* years.

Focus on items that increase your taxes without increasing your AGI. Check itemized deductions, like medical expenses. Group your medical expenses in non-base years, so taxes will be higher in base years and result in a lower EFC (*See also* p. 76-77.)

Social Security Tax Allowance

The Social Security Tax Allowance is calculated by applying the rates in Table A2 to the parents' and student's earned income.

Table A2: Social Security Tax	
Calculate separately the Social Security tax of father, mother, and student.	
Income Earned from Work*	**Social Security Tax**
$0 – $113,700	7.65% of income
$113,701 or greater	$8,698.05 + 1.45% of amount over $113,700
*Parent 1 (father/mother/stepparent) 2013 income earned from work is FAFSA/SAR #88. Parent 2 (father/mother/stepparent) 2013 income earned from work is FAFSA/SAR #89. Student's 2013 income earned from work is FAFSA/SAR #39. Social Security tax will never be less than zero.	

State and Other Tax Allowance

An allowance is computed for money spent on state and other taxes such as sales tax and property tax. The allowance is computed by taking the Total Income from the EFC worksheet and multiplying it by the applicable state tax rate shown in Table A1 for parents (p. 40) or Table A7 for students (p. 41).

Parents' tax rates have an income threshold. Parents with total income under $15,000 receive a higher rate. Parents with income bordering $15,000 might try to stay beneath this limit to qualify for the higher allowance to decrease their EFC. These parents might also apply for a means-tested federal benefit program to try to qualify for either the Automatic Zero or Simplified Needs Test.

Student's Legal Residence for the Base Years

Students are required to state on the FAFSA how long they lived in the current state. This answer will affect:

- Which state's rate is used when computing allowances deducted from the Expected Family Contribution *and*

- Which state receives the student's information (used to determine state financial aid)

If you are interested in state aid, be careful when deciding to relocate. Residing in any state for four years will meet any state's criteria for aid, but students who have not resided for four years will have to check their local eligibility requirements for aid.

Single, Separated, or Divorced Parents

In the case of single, separated, or divorced parents, when the custodial parent is the wealthier parent, parents might consider relocation, which in this case means a change of custody. Perhaps by junior year of high school, the student would relocate to live with the noncustodial parent, and thus be able to use this parents' lower income on the FAFSA.

As mentioned above, when relocation crosses states, parents should check each state's residency rules for state aid. It's possible moves in junior year will be too late, causing loss of state aid.

Change of custody changes other things as well. It reverses some dependency tax benefits associated with being a custodial parent.

Relocation isn't a decision to jump into lightly, but when there are rather large differences between custodial and noncustodial parent income, the possibility might be explored and comparisons of different scenarios could be made.

College Living Location

Aside from legal residence, students may also have to indicate whether they intend to live with parents, relatives, or roommates and on or off campus.

This information does not figure into the EFC calculations, but be aware that Institutional Financial Aid Advisors may use it when determining or adjusting the Cost of Attendance (COA) (*See* Professional Judgment p. 144). If the COA is adjusted, your financial need will be affected.

Table A1: State and Other Tax Allowance (Parents)
Note: $15,000 is a critical cut-off point for parents.

Table A1: State and Other Tax Allowance
for EFC Formula A Worksheet (parents only)

STATE	PERCENT OF TOTAL INCOME		STATE	PERCENT OF TOTAL INCOME	
	$0–$14,999	$15,000 or more		$0–$14,999	$15,000 or more
Alabama	3%	2%	Missouri	5%	4%
Alaska	2%	1%	Montana	5%	4%
American Samoa	2%	1%	Nebraska	5%	4%
Arizona	4%	3%	Nevada	3%	2%
Arkansas	4%	3%	New Hampshire	5%	4%
California	8%	7%	New Jersey	9%	8%
Canada and Canadian			New Mexico	3%	2%
Provinces	2%	1%	New York	9%	8%
Colorado	4%	3%	North Carolina	6%	5%
Connecticut	8%	7%	North Dakota	2%	1%
Delaware	5%	4%	Northern Mariana		
District of Columbia	7%	6%	Islands	2%	1%
Federated States			Ohio	5%	4%
of Micronesia	2%	1%	Oklahoma	3%	2%
Florida	3%	2%	Oregon	7%	6%
Georgia	5%	4%	Palau	2%	1%
Guam	2%	1%	Pennsylvania	5%	4%
Hawaii	4%	3%	Puerto Rico	2%	1%
Idaho	5%	4%	Rhode Island	7%	6%
Illinois	5%	4%	South Carolina	5%	4%
Indiana	4%	3%	South Dakota	2%	1%
Iowa	5%	4%	Tennessee	2%	1%
Kansas	5%	4%	Texas	3%	2%
Kentucky	5%	4%	Utah	5%	4%
Louisiana	3%	2%	Vermont	6%	5%
Maine	6%	5%	Virgin Islands	2%	1%
Marshall Islands	2%	1%	Virginia	6%	5%
Maryland	8%	7%	Washington	4%	3%
Massachusetts	7%	6%	West Virginia	3%	2%
Mexico	2%	1%	Wisconsin	7%	6%
Michigan	5%	4%	Wyoming	2%	1%
Minnesota	6%	5%	Blank or Invalid		
Mississippi	3%	2%	State	2%	1%
			OTHER	2%	1%

Multiply Parents' Total Income (EFC Formula A Worksheet, line 7) by the appropriate rate from the table above to get the "State and Other Tax Allowance" (EFC Formula A Worksheet, line 9). Use the parents' State of Legal Residence (FAFSA/SAR #70). If this item is blank or invalid, use the student's State of Legal Residence (FAFSA/SAR #18). If both items are blank or invalid, use the State in the Student's Mailing Address (FAFSA/SAR #6). If all three items are blank or invalid, use the rate for a blank or invalid state above.

Table A7: State and Other Tax Allowance (Students)
Note: Students have a flat rate.

Table A7: State and Other Tax Allowance
for EFC Formula A Worksheet (student only)

Alabama	2%	Missouri	3%
Alaska	0%	Montana	3%
American Samoa	2%	Nebraska	3%
Arizona	2%	Nevada	1%
Arkansas	3%	New Hampshire	1%
California	5%	New Jersey	4%
Canada and Canadian Provinces	2%	New Mexico	2%
Colorado	3%	New York	6%
Connecticut	5%	North Carolina	4%
Delaware	3%	North Dakota	1%
District of Columbia	5%	Northern Mariana Islands	2%
Federated States of Micronesia	2%	Ohio	3%
Florida	1%	Oklahoma	2%
Georgia	3%	Oregon	5%
Guam	2%	Palau	2%
Hawaii	3%	Pennsylvania	3%
Idaho	3%	Puerto Rico	2%
Illinois	2%	Rhode Island	4%
Indiana	3%	South Carolina	3%
Iowa	3%	South Dakota	1%
Kansas	3%	Tennessee	1%
Kentucky	4%	Texas	1%
Louisiana	2%	Utah	3%
Maine	4%	Vermont	3%
Marshall Islands	2%	Virgin Islands	2%
Maryland	5%	Virginia	4%
Massachusetts	4%	Washington	1%
Mexico	2%	West Virginia	3%
Michigan	3%	Wisconsin	4%
Minnesota	4%	Wyoming	1%
Mississippi	2%	Blank or Invalid State	2%
		OTHER	2%

Multiply the student's total income (EFC Formula A Worksheet, line 35) by the appropriate rate from the table above to get the "state and other tax allowance" (EFC Formula A Worksheet, line 37). Use the student's state of legal residence (FAFSA/SAR #18). If this item is blank or invalid, use the state in the student's mailing address (FAFSA/SAR #6). If both items are blank or invalid, use the parents' state of legal residence (FAFSA/SAR #70). If all three items are blank or invalid, use the rate for a blank or invalid state above.

Income Protection Allowance (IPA)

The Income Protection Allowance (IPA) is a deduction allowed for a family's basic daily living expenses for food, clothing, shelter, transportation, and so forth. Money must be spent on these items, so it isn't considered available for college or discretionary.

There is no consideration for where you live, despite the fact that obviously some places have a higher cost of living.

Parents use Table A3, Income Protection Allowance to figure the amount. This allowance varies based on the Household Size and the number of students attending college. (As you have more students in college, you receive less protection. The assumption is that your child is away at college, so your basic daily living expenses have gone down, and thus, you need less protection.)

Table A3: Income Protection Allowance

Number in parents' household, including student (FAFSA/SAR #73)	Number of college students in household (FAFSA/SAR #74)				
	1	2	3	4	5
2	$17,440	$14,460	—	—	—
3	21,720	18,750	$15,770	—	—
4	26,830	23,840	20,870	$17,890	—
5	31,650	28,670	25,700	22,710	$19,750
6	37,020	34,040	31,070	28,090	25,120

Note: For each additional family member, add $4,180.
For each additional college student (except parents), subtract $2,970.

The student Income Protection Allowance is a flat rate that changes each year. For the 2014-2015 application, the dependent student Income Protection Allowance is $6,260 and is already entered on the worksheet (*See* Line 39, p. 37).

The student allowance can also be used as a rough estimate of the amount a student could earn from work after taxes are withdrawn (take home pay) and not be expected to contribute income toward college expenses.

> *Example:* For the 2014-2015 application, if a student took home $6,260 after taxes, and has no other assets, this student is not expected to contribute *any of this income toward college.* The student portion of the EFC would be zero.

Household Size or Household Count

Household size factors into the Income Protection Allowance. **It always refers to the award year, not the base year.** When all other things are equal, larger households (meaning more people, not the square footage of the house) have higher expenses, and thus have less discretionary money. Consider two families with a $50,000 income, the family of four people is assumed to have more discretionary money than the family of six.

The student and parents are always part of the household size, unless a parent moved out as part of a separation or divorce, or if the student is independent (*See* p. 14). The student's siblings and student's children or any other person who receives more than half their support from the student's parents are also counted.

In an upcoming divorce, compare the effects of signing the FAFSA before the divorce which equates to a larger household size but possibly greater total income, to signing after the divorce where a working parent's income and assets would be excluded.

You can also include a child in the household when more than fifty percent of the child's support is paid by the parent, regardless of whether the child physically lives in the household.

New Baby

Children who will be born before the end of the award year, who will receive more than fifty percent of their support from their biological parent, will be the biological parents' dependent (for aid purposes), and included in the household count. If the student has or will have one or more children who receive more than half of their support from him or her between July 1, 2014 and June 30, 2015, this child is the student's dependent, and the student is an independent student.[18]

Death

In the event that the death of a family member is imminent, the FAFSA should be submitted before this, so this person is included in the household size.

---

18. EFC Formula Guide 2014-2015, *What is the Definition of Independent Student?*, p. 3, , http://ifap.ed.gov/efcformulaguide/attachments/091913EFC FormulaGuide1415.pdf

Employment Expense Allowance

The employment expense allowance is an allowance for work-related costs that *two working parents or a single parent* might incur, such as the need for a housekeeper, transportation, work clothes, or meals away from home. For the 2014-2015 school year:

- *For two working parents* (Parents' Marital Status is "married" or "unmarried and both parents living together"): the allowance is 35% of the lesser of the earned incomes or $4,000, whichever is less

- *For one-parent families:* the allowance is 35% of earned income, or $4,000, whichever is less

- *For two-parent families, with only one working parent:* zero allowance is permitted.[19]

Tip: Nonworking spouses might consider part time employment knowing up to $4,000 (35% of the first $11,428) in wages would not affect the family EFC.

Student Allowance for Parents' Negative Income

When parents' allowances are large enough to make the parents' Adjusted Available Income (AAI) negative, it is assumed the student must contribute to the family living expenses. To account for this, an Allowance for Parents' Negative Income is added in:

ALLOWANCES AGAINST STUDENT INCOME		
36. 2013 U.S. income tax paid (FAFSA/SAR #37) (tax filers only) If negative, enter zero.		
37. State and other tax allowance (Table A7) If negative, enter zero.	+	
38. Social Security tax allowance (Table A2)	+	
39. Income protection allowance	+	6,260
40. Allowance for parents' negative Adjusted Available Income (If line 25 is negative, enter line 25 as a positive number in line 40. If line 25 is zero or positive, enter zero in line 40.)	+	
41. TOTAL ALLOWANCES	=	

◀——— Allowance Adjustment

---

19. EFC Formula Guide 2014-2015, *Allowances Against Parent Income,* Question 13, p. 9, http://ifap.ed.gov/efcformulaguide/attachments/091913EFCFormulaGuide1415.pdf

We've discussed the shaded boxes below, Parent Income, Student Income, and deducted Allowances to arrive at Available Income.

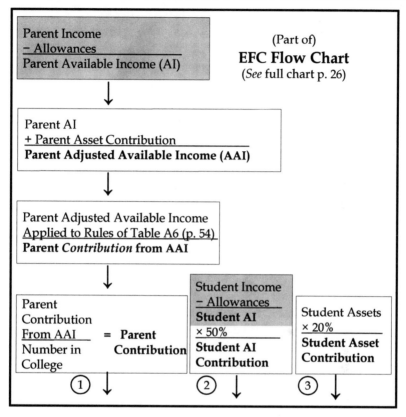

Student AI Contribution — Assessment of Student AI

Students are expected to contribute 50 percent of their Available Income toward college as shown in the lower (unshaded) section of the student income box above, and on line 43 below:

STUDENT'S CONTRIBUTION FROM INCOME		
Total income (from line 35)		
Total allowances (from line 41)	−	
42. Available income (AI)	=	
43. Assessment of AI	×	.50 ⟵
44. STUDENT'S CONTRIBUTION FROM AI If negative, enter zero.	=	

Employed Students

The general recommended work-hours for a college student to both work and obtain good grades ranges between 15 to 20 hours a week. Students should not work if their grades are suffering. After all, the intention is to work to pay for a college education. If the student is working but not learning, the reason for attending college is lost.

It would be a mistake for students to think working during their college years is not worthwhile. Quitting work does not always result in more aid (especially if earnings are under the amount protected by the student income allowance). (*See also* p. 137)

Some students qualify for Federal Work-Study (FWS) programs Work-study income *is not* included on the FAFSA. When asked on the FAFSA, if they are interested in work-study, students should always answer, "yes." This keeps the option open, but answering "yes" does not require the student to work.

Another good place for students to obtain employment is the family business (*See also* p. 56 and 75). When the business pays the student, this creates an expense, which means less profit to report on the family's tax form, a lower AGI, and a lower family EFC.

If these options are unavailable, a student can still obtain typical outside employment or become a self-employed entrepreneur.

Once a student's income *exceeds* the student's Total Allowances (*See* line 41 p. 44), the exceeded amount is assessed at 50 percent. When any income is saved, it becomes an asset which is assessed at 20 percent. (This is often referred to as the "Savers Penalty.") The end result is a student receives only 30 cents from every dollar worked in excess of Total Allowances.

> *Example:* A student earns $1.00 over the limit and saves it.
>
> $1.00 earned × 50 percent EFC income assessment = .50
> +$1.00 saved × 20 percent EFC asset assessment = .20
> Total amount claimed for EFC   = .70

> The student must contribute 70 cents (70 percent) of the earned *and saved* dollar toward the student EFC, or looked at another way, the student loses 70 cents in aid for every dollar earned and saved over the limit.

Note: the asset assessment can often be avoided by saving the earned income in a Roth IRA (*See* IRAs, p.72).

II. Assets for the EFC

The Regular EFC Worksheets include assets, defined as property that has an exchange value, including an investment, or investment farm or business.[20] Students who qualify for the Automatic Zero EFC or the Simplified Needs Test (SNT) do not have to be concerned with adjusting assets for *federal aid*, but these assets may still be used for awarding state or institutional aid.

Ownership of Assets

Ownership of assets can become quite complex. Further advice should be sought if you have any questions regarding assets that have part ownership, contested ownership, liens against property, foreclosures, or other unique circumstances.

Divorce Strategies for Assets — Overview

In cases of divorce, parents might plan ahead to ensure trusts, custodial accounts, and education accounts are in the name of the noncustodial parent, so they would not be reported as assets on the FAFSA. However, this idea usually backfires because distributions taken will count as income to the student assessed at the *student's income* assessment rate of 50 percent (*See* p. 100). Unless you can wait to take distributions until after signing the FAFSA for senior year of college, it is usually better to have the custodial parent own these accounts, to be assessed at the parent's rate.

Asset Assessment Rate — Overview

Parents are expected to contribute 12 percent of their assets (also called 12 percent of their discretionary net worth). As the formula is applied, this 12 percent is eventually reduced even further in a later step, to a maximum of 5.64 percent. (*See* p. 55)

Students are expected to contribute 20 percent of their assets (or net worth). (There is an exception for independent students with dependents other than spouse. They are assessed at 7 percent.)

If possible then, a strategy to increase financial need would be to keep assets in the parents' name, not the student's.

---

20. Application and Verification Guide 2013-2014, *Filling out the FAFSA*, "Income and Assets," p. 13, http://ifap.ed.gov/fsahandbook/attachments/1314AVGCh3.pdf

Excluded Assets

You might consider placing your savings in assets specifically excluded by the EFC formula. Per the Application and Verification Guide, these assets are not included in the formula:

1. Education Accounts owned by a third party (relatives, noncustodial parent, etc.) are excluded from assets.

2. Possessions (such as a car)

3. A family's principal place of residence is not reported, even if it is part of a business.
   — Try to finalize a home purchase prior to signing the FAFSA since the down payment and closing costs will reduce cash assets. (*See also* p. 64-65)

4. A family farm (including equipment, livestock, etc.) isn't reported as an investment on the FAFSA if:
   — It is the principal place of residence for the applicant and his family (spouse or, for dependent students, parents), and
   — The applicant (or parents of a dependent student) materially participated in the farming operation.

5. Family-owned and controlled small businesses (including farms) with 100 or fewer full-time or full-time equivalent employees do not count as an asset.
   — "Family-owned and controlled" means more than 50% of the business is owned by persons directly related or are/were related by marriage (members do not have to be part of the household count).

   * *Tip:* Starting a business may help shield assets and decrease income if it operates at a loss.

6. Retirement plans and Whole Life Insurance. 401(k) plans, pension funds, annuities, non-education IRAs, Keogh plans, cash value or equity in life insurance, and same year rollovers etc. — do not count.
   — *Note:* Distributions and/or insurance settlements do impact the EFC; count as *income* reported either in your AGI (if taxable) or as untaxed income.

7. Native American students: Property received under numerous different acts is excluded. (Check the guide.)

Included Assets

Cash, Savings, & Checking Accounts

All cash, including savings and checking accounts, is an asset.

Students may have money accumulated through gifts from grandparents, allowance, temporary employment, or some other source. This money is considered available for college use. It's worth repeating, that working students who are able to save their paychecks, should consider saving in a Roth IRA, so what is income this year, does not turn into an included assessed asset next year (*See* IRAs p. 72).

Spend the money now is a strategy often used to reduce assets. Before signing the FAFSA, you spend money that you planned to spend anyway in the upcoming year. Purchase college items, anything from a laundry bag to a microwave or even a car (paid with cash). Prepay auto insurance, purchase airfare needed to arrive at college, pay siblings' summer camp tuition, or complete home repairs. You could also pay off debt which decreases your assets and reduces interest payments. (Don't spend yourself down to zero though. You should have some emergency money.)

Small Business Net Worth

Parents and students who own an investment business or investment farm that does not fall under the exclusion rules, will report the net worth of the business or farm.

Parents (*not students*) are permitted a Net Worth Adjustment (reduction) for the value of their farm or business. This protects the business. This is calculated using Table A4.

Table A4: Business/Farm Net Worth Adjustment				
for EFC Formula A Worksheet (parents only)				
If the net worth of a business or farm is—	Then the adjusted net worth is—			
Less than $1	$0			
$1 to $125,000	40% of net worth of business/farm			
$125,001 to $375,000	$ 50,000	+	50%	of net worth over $125,000
$375,001 to $620,000	$175,000	+	60%	of net worth over $375,000
$620,001 or more	$322,000	+	100%	of net worth over $620,000

Other Assets

The following is a general list of included assets, with some tips to better position yourself. Some of these are discussed in further depth later, in their own sections:

1. Investments: Aim for a low AGI in base years.

   — Try to time the liquidation of your investments so capital gains will not show up in the base years.

   — Consider shifting investments out of dividend and capital gain bearing accounts, or invest in IRAs so *growth* does not affect your taxable income.

   — Consider selling bad investments to offset capital gains to reduce your taxable income reported.

   — Do not overvalue your investments. Use the most recent statements received or go online to obtain current prices. Print a copy for your records.

2. EE/I Bonds (*See* p. 97-99)

3. Qualified Tuition Plans (QTPs) not owned by a third party (*See* p. 100-103).

4. Trust Funds and Custodial Accounts (*See* p. 104-105):

   — In trust funds, a trustee manages an account for a beneficiary. Trusts are generally assets of the beneficiary unless they are restricted by a court order.

   — In custodial accounts, the custodian manages the account for the beneficiary (owner) who is a minor. Funds may be removed without penalty if used on the minor. Funds do not have to be used for college. These accounts are property of the owner (assets of the student) even though the student might gain control at age 18 or 21.

5. Rental Properties, in general, are income producing assets, not a business. A rental property business would have things like maid service, regular cleaning, and so forth.[21]

---

21. Application and Verification Guide 2013-2014, *Filling out the FAFSA*, "Rental Properties," p. 15, http://ifap.ed.gov/fsahandbook/attachments/1314AVG.pdf

Education Savings and Asset Protection Allowance

Parents are permitted an Asset Protection Allowance (deduction) using Table A5 to arrive at a discretionary net worth. This is an amount of assets, based on the age of the older parent, that parents can accumulate before they are expected to contribute toward college expenses.

It's possible this amount could zero out all your assets. If this is the case, you would have *no need to shift your assets* around until you begin to exceed this allowance.

Table A5: Parents' Education Savings and Asset Protection Allowance
for EFC Formula A Worksheet (parents only)

Age of older parent as of 12/31/2014*	Allowance if there are two parents**	Allowance if there is only one parent	Age of older parent as of 12/31/2014*	Allowance if there are two parents**	Allowance if there is only one parent
25 or less	$0	$0	45	$30,700	$7,100
26	1,800	400	46	31,500	7,200
27	3,600	800	47	32,200	7,400
28	5,500	1,300	48	33,000	7,600
29	7,300	1,700	49	33,800	7,800
30	9,100	2,100	50	34,600	8,000
31	10,900	2,500	51	35,700	8,100
32	12,700	2,900	52	36,500	8,300
33	14,600	3,400	53	37,600	8,500
34	16,400	3,800	54	38,500	8,700
35	18,200	4,200	55	39,700	9,000
36	20,000	4,600	56	40,600	9,200
37	21,800	5,000	57	41,800	9,400
38	23,700	5,500	58	43,000	9,700
39	25,500	5,900	59	44,200	9,900
40	27,300	6,300	60	45,500	10,200
41	27,900	6,500	61	46,800	10,400
42	28,500	6,600	62	48,100	10,700
43	29,200	6,800	63	49,500	11,000
44	30,000	6,900	64	50,900	11,300
			65 or over ..	52,600	11,600

*Determine the age of the older parent listed in FAFSA/SAR #64 and #68 as of 12/31/2014. If no parent date of birth is provided, use age 45.

**Use the two parent allowance when the Parents' Marital Status listed in FAFSA/SAR #59 is "married or remarried" or "unmarried and both parents living together."

The student does not have an Asset Protection Allowance, which is another reason to keep assets in the parents' name. For the federal formula Regular Worksheet, as soon as the student has $1 in assets (net worth), the student is expected to use part of that toward college.

Three Differences between Student and Parent Assets

There are three differences between student and parent assets. The student has:

1. No Adjustment for Net Worth of a business or farm

2. No Education Savings and Asset Protection Allowance

3. Net worth assessed at the rate of 20 percent

Parent Contribution from Assets

PARENTS' CONTRIBUTION FROM ASSETS		
16. Cash, savings & checking (FAFSA/SAR #90)		
17. Net worth of investments** (FAFSA/SAR #91) If negative, enter zero.		
18. Net worth of business and/or investment farm (FAFSA/SAR #92) If negative, enter zero.		
19. Adjusted net worth of business/farm (Calculate using Table A4.)	+	← ①
20. **Net worth** (sum of lines 16, 17, and 19)	=	
21. Education savings and asset protection allowance (Table A5)	–	← ②
22. Discretionary net worth (line 20 minus line 21)	=	
23. Asset conversion rate	×	.12 ←
24. **CONTRIBUTION FROM ASSETS** If negative, enter zero.	=	

Student Contribution from Assets

STUDENT'S CONTRIBUTION FROM ASSETS		
45. Cash, savings & checking (FAFSA/SAR #41)		③
46. Net worth of investments* (FAFSA/SAR #42) If negative, enter zero.		
47. Net worth of business and/or investment farm (FAFSA/SAR #43) If negative, enter zero.	+	
48. **Net worth** (sum of lines 45 through 47)	=	
49. Assessment rate	×	.20 ←
50. **STUDENT'S CONTRIBUTION FROM ASSETS**	=	

At this point, we're about half-way done. We've discussed the shaded areas on the flow chart below:

- Parent Available Income (AI)
    - Taxable income, exclusions, additions, and offsets
    - Allowances subtracted from Parent Income
- Parent Assets Contribution
- Parent Adjusted Available Income (AAI)
- Student Available Income (AI)
    - Taxable income, exclusions, additions and offsets
    - Allowances subtracted from Student Income
    - Student Income Assessment Rate of 50 percent
- Student Assets
    - Student Asset Assessment Rate of 20 percent

Parent Contribution from AAI is discussed next.

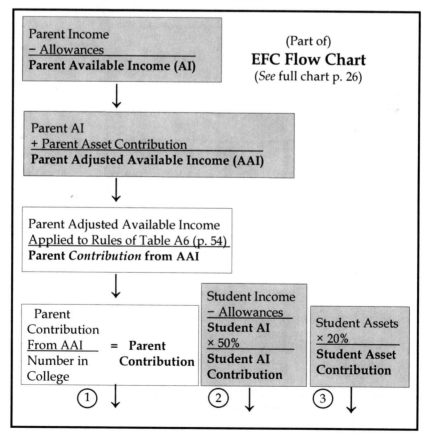

Parent Contribution from AAI

Parents' contribution from Adjusted Available Income (AAI) is determined by applying the formula from Table A6 as shown in the flow chart and tables below. As you can see the percentage applied ranges from a flat $750 to 47 percent of AAI.

> Parent Adjusted Available Income (AAI)
> Applied to Rules of Table A6 (below)
> **Parent *Contribution* from AAI**

The result is entered on the Dependent Student, Regular EFC Worksheet, line 26:

PARENTS' CONTRIBUTION		
AVAILABLE INCOME (AI) (from line 15)		
CONTRIBUTION FROM ASSETS (from line 24)	+	
25. **Adjusted Available Income (AAI)** May be a negative number.	=	
26. **Total parents' contribution from AAI** (Calculate using Table A6.) If negative, enter zero.		←
27. **Number in college in 2014–2015** (Exclude parents) (FAFSA/SAR #74)	÷	
28. **PARENTS' CONTRIBUTION** (standard contribution for nine-month enrollment)*** If negative, enter zero.	=	

Table A6: Parents' Contribution from AAI

If parents' AAI is—			The parents' contribution from AAI is—			
Less than -$3,409			-$750			
-$3,409	to	$15,600	22% of AAI			
$15,601	to	$19,600	$3,432	+	25% of AAI over	$15,600
$19,601	to	$23,500	$4,432	+	29% of AAI over	$19,600
$23,501	to	$27,500	$5,563	+	34% of AAI over	$23,500
$27,501	to	$31,500	$6,923	+	40% of AAI over	$27,500
$31,501 or more			$8,523	+	47% of AAI over	$31,500

Parent Asset Assessment Rate of 5.64 Percent

Often articles will discuss the fact that parents are always assessed at a lower rate than students. Many times the article will use the figure of 5.64 percent and occasionally, the article says something like, "Parent assets are assessed at a maximum of 5.64 percent."

This can be confusing if you have begun to educate yourself on the rules for completing the FAFSA and computing the EFC. As shown previously, parents' assets (discretionary net worth) are assessed at 12 percent (line 23 p.52), so why the talk of a maximum of 5.64 percent?

The articles are taking the formula one step further, applying the rules of Table A6. The maximum Parents' Contribution from AAI assessment percentage on Table A6 is 47 percent and 47 percent of 12 percent equals 5.64 percent.

You can also see this in the flowchart:

Parent AI
+ Parent Asset Contribution
Parent Adjusted Available Income (AAI)

This could be written as:

Parent AI
+ 12% of discretionary net worth
Parent Adjusted Available Income (AAI)

Apply Table A6 rules to each component as shown to arrive at parent contribution from AAI:

Parent AI   × Maximum Rate of 47%
+ 12% of Discretionary Net Worth × Maximum Rate of 47%
Parent *Contribution from* AAI

This reduces to show the 5.64 percent, the actual assessment rate often referred to for *parent assets.*

**Parents' Actual
Asset Assessment
(Maximum Rate)** →
Parent AI × a Maximum Rate of 47%
+ 5.64% of Asset Contribution
Parent *Contribution from* AAI

Some Parent Asset Strategies

1. **Save in the parents' name:** The parents' asset assessment percentage is always lower than the student's, so keep assets attributable to the parents.

2. **Use the family business to shelter more assets:** The family business can employ the student, which creates the earned income required to shield up to $5,500 (for 2013 or 2014) in a student Roth IRA. This is an asset in the student's name, but nevertheless, a shielded asset.

3. **Spend the money:** Spend the student's assets (money) first and also consider skipping a loan and spending assets.

   Example: A student has $10,000 in assets and the parents' have $5,000 in a savings account. Both sources are discretionary money and the student needs $10,000 for college.

   Acceptable option 1: The student spends $5,000 and takes a loan for $5,000. Next year the student and parent will each have $5,000 in assets ($10,000 total) counting against the family for financial aid.

   Acceptable option 2: The student and parents each spend $5,000. Next year the student's $5,000 in assets counts against the family for financial aid.

   Acceptable option 3: The student spends $10,000. Next year the parents will have $5,000 in assets counting against the family for financial aid.

Option 3 is clearly better than Option 2, because parent assets are assessed at a lower rate and only the parents' $5,000 is left for the following year's FAFSA assessment. Usually Option 3 is better than Option 1 for the same reason. Additionally, in all three solutions the loan debt and interest are avoided for this year.

An exception might be when a family needs access to cash, such as in cases of job loss. When there is a reason to preserve cash, perhaps, Option 1 would be the best choice. Choosing between Option 1 and 3 really depends on your personal finances.

III. Students in College

The Parents' Contribution from Adjusted Available Income (AAI) is divided by the number of students in college to arrive at the Parent Contribution. (Recall, that the number of students in college also impacted the Income Protection Allowance (IPA) (*See* p. 42)).

$$\frac{\text{Parent Contribution From AAI}}{\text{Number in College}} = \text{Parent Contribution}$$

PARENTS' CONTRIBUTION		
AVAILABLE INCOME (AI) (from line 15)		
CONTRIBUTION FROM ASSETS (from line 24)	+	
25. **Adjusted Available Income (AAI)** May be a negative number.	=	
26. **Total parents' contribution from AAI** (Calculate using Table A6.) If negative, enter zero.		
27. **Number in college in 2014–2015** (Exclude parents) (FAFSA/SAR #74)	÷	
28. **PARENTS' CONTRIBUTION** (standard contribution for nine-month enrollment)*** If negative, enter zero.	=	

Who to count for this entry is defined as:

"The applicant is always included in the number in college, but parents are not included. Others who count in the household size are in the number in college if they are or will be enrolled at least half time during the award year in an eligible degree or certificate program at a school eligible for any of the FSA programs. The definition of half-time enrollment for this question must meet the federal requirements even if the school defines half time differently. Do not include students at a U.S. service academy because most of their primary educational expenses are paid for by the federal government.."[22]

---

22. Application and Verification Guide 2013-2014, *Filling out the FAFSA*, "Number in College," p. 27, http://ifap.ed.gov/fsahandbook/attachments/1314AVG.pdf

Conceiving Children

In general, the more students in college — the greater the aid. This is good news for families who have conceived twins, triplets, or children close together.

The common idea to conceive children several years apart in order to "afford the college years" actually results in the *family* (not federal aid) paying for more of the overall college expenses.

This concept is similar to paying for a car. It will always be cheaper to pay the car off quickly rather than over a period of time, but each person has to decide whether the greater monthly payments are actually affordable.

Conceiving children several years apart spreads out the college years. Two children conceived four years apart results in eight years of college payments. If they were conceived two years apart, the parents would have only six years of college payments.

Six years of college payments results in more aid because the Parents' Contribution from AAI is *divided by the number of students currently in college*, but it also results in more stress on the family finances because two college payments must be made at once.

Delaying College

Parents who have already conceived their children still have options surrounding the Number of Students in College aspect of the financial aid formula.

A family with two children four years apart, might decide the older child should delay starting college for one or two years, thus creating some overlap whereby two children would attend college during the same year, and thus qualify for additional aid.

Keep in mind, if a student does delay college and chooses to work, this student's full-time income will then impact the family EFC. It would be much better for a student who chooses to delay attending college to do something else, like volunteer abroad.

School Aid Forms and the PROFILE

The explanations thus far refer to the Federal Methodology (FM). Some schools use their own Institutional Methodology (IM) rules or use the College Scholarship Service (CSS) PROFILE form to award their own additional aid. The PROFILE costs $25 for the application and $16 each time the information is sent to a school. Fee waivers are automatically generated for qualifying families.

Ask your schools ahead of time what additional items they consider. If you add school codes to your PROFILE and work through to the end, you will also see a list of schools and each question they asked for. PROFILE and school aid forms might:

1. Include excluded assets such as the home equity of your primary residence, the value of retirement accounts, and the cash value of life insurance policies

2. Ask for all Educational Accounts where the student is a beneficiary, even if owned by a third party

3. Add assets of siblings, including all educational accounts naming them as beneficiary

4. Add a Schedule C small business loss back into the AGI (preventing you from using a small business loss to qualify for more aid) or ask for balance sheet information

5. Use different assessment rates for income and assets

6. Ask about assistance received from relatives

7. Include pre-tax contributions held from wages, including Flexible Spending Arrangements (accounts) (FSAs)

8. Include EIC and the Additional Child Tax Credit

9. Ask when a car was purchased (A recent purchase might be included as money that was available for college.)

10. Reduce the COA for scholarships already awarded

These changes only affect the award of aid from the school itself, not federal aid, so if you've made adjustments based on the federal EFC rules, you have not lost any opportunity to receive federal awards.

Is Shielding Assets Important?

There are three good reasons to be cautious shifting assets:

1. If parent assets are low enough, they could be zeroed out by the Education Savings and Asset Protection Allowance (*See* p. 51) and parents would have no need to shield them. (Students do not have this allowance. All assets in a student's name are assessed at 20 percent.)

2. You also have no need to shield assets if you qualify for the Automatic Zero EFC or the Simplified Needs Test.

3. You may want easy access to your assets, and if so, they should not all be in shielded in accounts that may have penalties for withdrawals.

If you choose not to shield assets, try to always save in the parents name since the parent's assets are assessed at a maximum rate of 5.64 percent and the student's are assessed at 20 percent.

Since the bulk of the EFC comes from income, student income assessed at 50 percent and parents' income assessed at rates up to 47 percent (*See* p.54), you might examine whether shifting your assets will be worthwhile. Figure out how your assets impact your EFC.

> *Example:* For every $10,000 in parent assets, the EFC will rise by $564 ($10,000 × 5.64 percent) and for every $10,000 in student assets the EFC will rise by $2,000 ($10,000 × 20 percent).
>
> — Is $564 less aid important to you?
>
>> * Multiply it by four years and it's $2,256 in aid.
>> * If you have $20,000 in assets, the decrease in aid over four years will be $4,512.
>
> — Is $2,000 less aid important to you?
>
>> * Multiply it by four, so it's really $8,000 in aid.
>> * If the student has $20,000 in assets, the decrease in aid over four years will be $16,000.

If you run the numbers for your family assets, you can make an educated decision as to whether shielding assets is worthwhile.

Is Adjusting Income Important?

The EFC is derived from a mixture of income and assets (and the number of students in college). It is definitely better to have low income with high assets, than to have high income and low assets. At first glance, you might think income cannot be influenced.

Remember that for the Automatic Zero EFC and the Simplified Needs Test (SNT), income refers to your Adjusted Gross Income (AGI) on your tax return.

This is different from the Available Income (AI) used on the Regular EFC formula Worksheet. Recall that AI as defined is much greater than your earned income: you add in untaxed income and certain benefits, and subtract out certain allowances (*See* p. 26-46).

Your first goal should be to focus on your AGI to try to qualify for the Automatic Zero EFC or the Simplified Needs Test. Perhaps you think your income is nowhere near the thresholds of $24,000 and $49,999, but take a second look. Can your AGI be reduced by using Flexible Spending Accounts, employer retirement plans, changing investments, or some other line on the front of your tax form? Should you get rid of Capital Gains by changing your investments? If both parents contribute the maximum amount to a deductible IRA, AGI reduces by $10,000. What else is possible?

To qualify for these special EFC categories (*See* p. 18 & 22) you must receive designated benefits or be eligible to file a 1040A or 1040EZ. Find out if you *really* have to file the Form 1040. Can you make adjustment to avoid filing the long form during base years?

Striving to meet the criteria for an Automatic Zero not only excludes your family assets and income, but it allows your student to work during college for any salary and this income will not be assessed at all. You're doing more than eliminating your EFC.

Meeting SNT rules excludes both the parents' and student's assets from EFC calculations. The impact isn't as momentous as qualifying for a zero EFC, but it's certainly significant.

Even if you cannot adjust to qualify for one of the special EFC categories, you can still aim to make adjustments to your Available Income (AI) computed on the Regular EFC Worksheet. Review included and excluded income items and every allowance permitted to be deducted to see what might be modified. Try to decrease your AGI, increase your allowances and excluded income, or decrease your untaxed income and benefits.

Lost Opportunity Cost (LOC)

When you make a withdrawal from a savings or other account that has the potential for growth, you will always have a *Lost Opportunity Cost (LOC)*. You lose the opportunity for growth on the funds you withdrew.

> *Example:* Morgan, age 17, works in her parents' business, and has contributed $300 every year, for 10 years to her retirement fund, a Roth IRA. Her contributions total $3,000 ($300 × 10 years). During her senior year of high school, Morgan has a balance of $3,962 in her Roth IRA ($3,000 from contributions and $962 in earnings). She can withdraw her contributions for any reason, at any time, without paying a penalty or taxes.
>
> Morgan withdraws $3,000 for college. She has now lost the future compound earnings and tax-free growth on this $3,000. Morgan wants to know how much she lost. Online at http://www.moneychimp.com/calculator/ compound_interest_calculator.htm, she enters $3,000, 5 percent for an estimated rate, and 48 for the number of years until she would retire. The result is $31,203.81! If Morgan had not made a withdrawal and let her money grow, compounding at 5 percent, she would have had $31,203.81 at retirement time.
>
> Morgan should understand withdrawing $3,000 caused not a $3,000 loss, but a $31,203.81 lost opportunity cost.

When the decision comes to pay for college, you will decide if you will take the path of a lost opportunity cost by pulling from your assets, or take the path of an interest cost by taking a loan. In most cases, it will be a mixture of both.

Remember, there is always a cost factor when you spend money and it's *always* more than the price of the item itself.

There are only two ways to pay for something:

1. You pull from savings, creating a Lost Opportunity Cost, or

2. You take a loan, which results in interest payments

Smart Decisions, Don't Forget the FAFSA Rules

Choosing between a Lost Opportunity Cost and interest payments would be easy if you only had to think about rates. On a typical purchase, when your a stock earns 5 percent and your loan interest is 3 percent, you take a loan because the stock rate exceeds the loan rate; you are ahead 2 percent (5 percent − 3 percent). With a college purchase, there is one more factor, the FAFSA rules.

Example: A student with $10,000 asset earning 5 percent interest plans to withdraw $2,000 for college. The EFC assessment computed to $2,000 ($10,000 × 20 percent). The student has a need of $2,000 and is offered a loan at 3 percent interest. Should the student take the loan or withdraw *another* $2,000 from assets to pay expenses?

Compare the student EFC across two years with two options:

	No Loan	Loan
Student Assets	$10,000	$10,000
Student withdraws $2,000 (EFC From Assets = Assets × 20%)	$ 2,000	$ 2,000
Assets Remaining	$ 8,000	$ 8,000
Decline the loan (Withdraw another $2,000 from Assets)	$ 2,000	
Take the Loan		$ 2,000
Loan Interest of 3%		$ 60
Asset Remaining	$ 6,000	$ 8,000
Next Year Asset Value (after 5% interest applied)	$ 6,300	$ 8,400
Next Year **Student EFC From Assets = Assets × 20%**	$ 1,260	$ 1,680

By not taking a loan, the student avoids the $60 in interest, but more importantly, the EFC is reduced by $420 ($1,680-$1,260) which creates a greater financial need. This need should result in additional aid, preferably free aid or work-study.

This student should decline a loan and spend student assets.

Home Equity

Home equity is another place where the FAFSA rules may appear unfair. Compare the following example:

> *Example:* Single dad Michael rents his apartment. Single dad Joe has a home with equity of $50,000. All other factors are the same. These two dads will have the same Expected Family Contribution.

The explanation behind this thought process is unclear. Perhaps the idea is you should not have to sacrifice your home for the student to attend school. Regardless of the logic, families aware of the home equity rule can use it to their advantage. Knowing the law will also help you explain to your student why a friend living in a *mansion* receives equal or even more financial aid.

Your primary residence can be a good place to shield assets. Home equity does not count for the federal EFC calculation. If you have spare cash available that will count as an included asset for the EFC, you should consider paying off more of your home mortgage, assuming there are no prepayment penalties.

When you answer questions about the value of your home, you should state what it would sell for as of today. You can take into consideration the current economy, what you would pay a realtor, and subtract the cost of repairs you would have to complete prior to selling (painting, driveway resurfacing, gutter cleaning, appliance or utility replacements, etc.). It is important to not overstate this figure. Keep a written record of your valuation.

If you have been saving up for a home purchase, you might plan to close on a home prior to signing the FAFSA. This will remove the down payment from your savings account (an included asset) and turn it into home equity (an excluded asset) for federal aid. Since home equity *is counted* by some schools for awarding aid directly from the school, it is important to realize you are only shifting an asset for federal aid purposes.

If you are applying to a school that does consider the net worth of your home in its own aid calculations, you might try to decrease the equity of your home. You can also use these strategies to decrease equity in a second home, such as a summer cottage.

When trying to reduce home equity on either your primary residence or a secondary residence, consider the following:

a. *Home Repair:* Take a home equity loan to complete a necessary home repair that you may have been putting off. Your home equity goes down for a repair you planned to do anyway.

b. *Shifting Debt:* Credit card debt and car loans do not help you receive more financial aid. Consider taking a home equity loan to pay off these types of debt. Home equity goes down.

If the home equity loan is from a second home, reducing equity impacts the federal formula. If the loan is from your primary residence, it might impact school aid, depending on the school.

The general term "home equity loan" can mean: a home equity loan, a second mortgage, or a home equity line of credit. For FAFSA purposes, the line of credit is best. With a line of credit, you access it only as needed. It is similar to your ability to take a cash advance on a credit card. The money is there if you need it.

With a loan, you must receive the loan amount in full and hold it somewhere awaiting use. This loan amount being held, will be an included asset assessed each year for financial aid purposes.

If you have two homes, always take the home equity line of credit on the secondary residence first, because that home is counted for federal aid. Some advantages of home equity loans or lines of credit are:

1. You may receive a tax write off for the interest.

2. Home equity itself is not growing. The value of your house increases (or decreases) whether you have equity in it or not, so why not take advantage of home equity?

3. They usually have a low interest rate.

There are disadvantages too. If you decide to access your home equity, you should be prepared for larger monthly payments or you might try to refinance to keep your monthly payments the same. Touching home equity for college is similar to touching retirement funds for college. You are dipping into money that should be used for your own security. Before you pull a home equity loan to pay for college, perhaps reconsider cheaper schools to be sure the education is worth the additional debt incurred.

After-tax or Tax-equivalent Rate

When you hear talk of the "after-tax rate" or "tax-equivalent rate" or yields being tax-exempt, it really comes down to one concept. Your dollars are earning a higher rate because you are not paying taxes on them. The higher rate will depend on the tax bracket you are in.

The following formula is used to compute a tax-exempt yield:

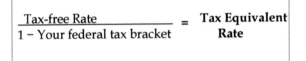

$$\frac{\text{Tax-free Rate}}{1 - \text{Your federal tax bracket}} = \begin{array}{c}\textbf{Tax Equivalent} \\ \textbf{Rate}\end{array}$$

The greater your tax bracket, the greater your savings in a tax-free account.

Example: A tax-free fund earns 1 percent. If you are in the 28 percent tax bracket, your tax equivalent rate is:

$$\frac{1}{1 - .28} = 1.39\%$$

If you are in the 15 percent tax bracket, your tax equivalent rate is:

$$\frac{1}{1 - .15} = 1.18\%$$

In this example, if you were in the 15 percent tax bracket and you had a choice of an investment that earns 1 percent tax-free and an investment that earns 1.2 percent, the better choice is the 1.2 percent investment, even though you will pay taxes on it.

Just because an investment is tax-free doesn't mean it's the best. You have to look at the rates of return and your tax bracket. If you are in a lower tax bracket, you should pay close attention to someone *selling you* an investment based on after-tax rates. Make sure calculations are accomplished using your true tax bracket.

Pensions and Retirement Accounts

Retirement funds are not college savings accounts, even if they have some special features to make withdrawals for education.

Retirement accounts are an excluded asset for the federal EFC formula, so another way to shield your assets is to fully fund your retirement accounts.

Think of your family budget, in which you have so much designated for food, so much for the mortgage or rent, and so much for clothing. You are really not supposed to use mortgage or rent money to purchase clothing. Even though you can, it doesn't mean you should, and when you do, there are consequences (perhaps mortgage late fees or credit card interest).

The same thing happens if you use retirement money for college expenses; there will be consequences: a Lost Opportunity Cost.

If you don't have money for college, you can almost always obtain a loan, but if you don't have money at retirement time, you can't take a loan to retire.

Some advantages of retirement accounts are:

1. You are saving for your own retirement.

2. You are shielding money from the EFC formula.

3. You have no restriction on how funds may be used.

4. You may be able to participate using pre-tax dollars.

5. You may receive tax-deferred or tax-free growth.

6. You have a dire emergency source for college expenses.

For financial aid purposes, the main attraction of retirement accounts is their excluded asset status. By placing money in these accounts, you not only take care of your retirement, but you reduce your EFC.

Also, consider how some other investments are restricted to be used only for eligible educational expenses. What happens when your student receives a full scholarship? This isn't necessarily an awful problem. At least the problem is how to spend the money. At least there is money. But with retirement accounts, there are no restrictions for fund use, so you will never have this dilemma.

Some people think retirement accounts should not be shielded, and they are another loophole in the EFC computation.

> *Example:* Family A has $10,000 in retirement funds and Family B has $100,000 in retirement funds. All other factors are the same. These two families will have the same Expected Family Contribution.

Two viewpoints on this scenario are:

1. Retirement funds should be spent on college

    — Family B with $100,000 deserves less aid because it can use the retirement funds for college.

2. Government aid *should be* used to help fund retirements

    — Family A needs to save for retirement *and* pay for college, where as Family B only needs to pay for college. Giving Family A more aid will allow it to spend less on college and save more for retirement. (The net result is government funding is indirectly helping fund the retirement account.)

There is no easy answer, which is why shielding of retirement funds continues to be a debatable topic. But for now, until the government changes it, they are shielded assets, so let's use them.

Retirement accounts should be a last resort, the last place to pull funds to pay college expenses. Last resort means, *dire need.* The student will be attending the cheapest college, living at home, riding a bike, and eating peanut butter sandwiches for dinner. You can't even afford the jelly. (This is how important it should be to you—to not touch and to protect your retirement accounts.)

If the current situation is so dire that you will pull money from these accounts, how dismal will it be when you retire?

Sometimes parents decide to ignore this concept. The love of the child and desire to *please and provide* has won priority over the parents' nice future nursing home. Long term plans are changed.

The new plan is for the parents to sacrifice, to either retire later (work longer), or perhaps in the elderly years, to skip the nursing home and instead, move in with the student.

Do parents explain this last option to the student? Probably not; probably because the parents aren't thinking about the long-term consequences: how retirement distributions will create problems.

Distributions

The first problem with taking withdrawals (distributions) from retirement funds is you are liquidating an excluded asset and turning it into an included income and/or asset for the EFC.

Because of this, you should never take a withdrawal before signing the FAFSA. Take it after the FAFSA submission and spend it entirely before signing the next FAFSA. This will avoid the withdrawal as counting as an asset for aid.

You're not out of the woods yet. You still have to consider the income effects. Distributions count as income, appearing in the AGI if taxable or as untaxed income if nontaxable. (*See* p. 33 & 48) Distributions will affect your EFC for the following year.

Think about this. You are in *dire need* so you withdraw from your retirement funds. Now, you've increased your EFC for next year, so next year you will need even more money. You are in *more dire need* and have to withdraw from retirement funds again.

Wait! *Dire need* was supposed to be the limit. You were not supposed to have *more dire need* and *even more dire need,* and so forth. Touching your retirement funds will only force you to touch them again and again and again.

Save in a Retirement Account or College Fund?

"How do I choose?" a parent asks. "I'm limited on funds. Do I save for college or retirement first?"

Even if you didn't take to heart the point about how *you can borrow for college, but you can't borrow to retire*, there is a second point to justify why you always save for retirement first:

When you save for retirement, *you are saving for college.*

Remember every dollar you save in a retirement fund decreases the family EFC and increases the aid a student will receive. When you save for retirement, you are creating money for the student. If funds are limited, fund your retirement account and sleep well because you know you are helping your student. (*See also,* p. 128)

Employer Matching Pre-tax Plans and Penalties

This book focuses on how investments are viewed by the EFC formula, but growth and return on investment cannot be ignored. In most cases, you will want to fund an employer matching plan first, before an IRA and before any college savings investment.

Usually an employer matching retirement plan is a dollar-for-dollar match up to a maximum dollar amount or percent of your salary. This means if you contribute $1,000, your employer will also contribute $1,000 to the account. Because of this 100 percent rate of return, employer matching plans are usually the first investment choice for a family. Working students should also inquire and participate in a company plan if available.

If you are eligible, the employer matching plan should be funded first, at least up to the employer match figure.

> *Example:* Employees are permitted to contribute $8,000 to an employer matching plan. The employer will match the first $3,000. The employee should fund the initial $3,000. After that, the employee should compare the employer plan with other investment choices.

When opening a pension or retirement plan, ask if the account is employer matching, how it's invested (stocks, mutual funds, etc.), what the withdrawal rules are (when and how often they can be made) and if they have any penalties or fees associated with withdrawals, rollovers, or transfers.

Pre-tax retirement contributions, such as those made to company retirement plans, are considered money available for the base year. The retirement fund shields the money from being declared as an asset in future year calculations, but for those using the Regular formula, it is still *Available Income* during the year it was contributed.

> *Example:* Your $60,000 taxable income does not include the $3,000 pre-tax dollars contributed to your employer retirement plan. The Regular formula will base your EFC on $63,000 ($60,000 AGI + $3,000).

Contributions to the employer plan does reduce your AGI on your tax return and some families will be able to use this feature to qualify for either the Automatic Zero EFC or the Simplified Needs Test, discussed next.

Pre-tax, Tax Deferment, or Deductible Plans

Contributions to a pre-tax employer plan, Keoghs, 401(k)s, 403bs, or traditional IRAs are *added* to your AGI in the EFC computation. However, these plans may reduce your AGI enough to qualify for the Automatic Zero EFC or Simplified Needs Test (SNT). Remember AGI is used for these tests, not Available Income (AI).

> *Example SNT:* Parents with an AGI of $53,000 meet all the requirements for the SNT except for AGI. If they contribute $3,001 or more to a pre-tax employer plan (or a traditional IRA), they will reduce their AGI below $50,000 and qualify for the Simplified Needs Test. While their contribution *will be added* to their AGI for calculating their EFC, they have just *excluded all their assets* from the EFC (because they qualified for the SNT).

> *Example Automatic Zero EFC:* Parents with an AGI of $25,000 decide to contribute $2,000 to a traditional IRA (or pre-tax employer plan) to bring their AGI below the $24,000 limit. This family now qualifies for the Automatic Zero EFC. The IRA contribution is *not* added back into calculations because there is no EFC to calculate; their EFC is automatically zero.

Flexible Spending Arrangements (FSAs)

Flexible Spending Arrangements (FSAs) or Flexible Spending Accounts, are employer pre-tax programs for day-care, meal plans, or medical (including dental programs). Contributions to and payments from these accounts are *excluded* from income. They can be used as described above: to reduce AGI, perhaps even enough to qualify for an Automatic Zero EFC or SNT.

Health Savings Accounts (HSAs)

Health Savings Accounts (HSAs) are medical savings plans that follow rules similar to retirement plans. Prior to retirement, they have penalties for withdrawals not used for medical expenses. The balance is not an asset for EFC. These accounts could be loaded to reduce your AGI.

Note: Distributions and contributions outside of your payroll may force you to file a 1040 which could make you ineligible for the Automatic Zero or SNT, unless you meet other rules.

Individual Retirement Accounts (IRAs)

Individual Retirement Accounts (IRAs) will not give you the guaranteed dollar-for-dollar return of an employer matching plan, but they should be considered once the employer match amount has been met. It may be wiser to stop contributing to the employer plan at the employer match amount and begin an IRA.

All IRA contributions become shielded, excluded assets for the EFC. This is the primary reason to use them.

There are two types of IRAs: a Traditional and a Roth. The most you can contribute to one or more IRAs for 2013 and 2014 is $5,500 ($6,500 if over age 50). You have until the tax-filing deadline to contribute for that tax year and you must have *earned income* to contribute. (Nonworking spouses can use their working spouse's income to qualify. Ex-spouses should be aware that alimony does count as eligible income for IRA contributions.)

Qualified distributions are permitted after you have had at least one account opened for five years, so it is important to open an account, even if you only contribute $100 the first year. Distributions made from an IRA before age 59½ incur taxes and a penalty. After age 59½ you will pay only taxes; no penalty.

IRAs have a special exception rule for distributions used for qualified educational expenses. Up to $10,000 may be withdrawn from an IRA before age 59½ and you pay only taxes; no penalty, but consider this option carefully. There is a reason they are called *retirement* accounts and not college savings accounts.

Traditional IRA

If you meet eligibility rules, Traditional IRA contributions are tax deductible and lower your AGI, which may help you qualify for either the Automatic Zero EFC or the Simplified Needs Test. A family that in January deposits $5,500 in both a 2013 and 2014 IRA for each parent will create a $11,000 AGI reduction and $22,000 asset reduction prior to signing the FAFSA.

Traditional IRA accounts grow tax-deferred. Distributions are allocated proportionately, some will be considered contributions (basis) and some will be considered gains, but the *entire* distribution is counted as income for the EFC computations.

Around age 70½, you are *required* to make withdrawals called Required Mandatory Distributions (RMDs). If your RMDs occur in FAFSA base years, they will impact your EFC. Distributions count as income. (How do you like the government deciding at what age you *can* withdraw money and at what age you *must* withdraw your money?)

This is not to imply that IRAs are bad. They are an excellent tax-deferred investment opportunity — with some weaknesses.

Older parents can avoid Required Mandatory Withdrawals (RMDs) by converting traditional IRAs into a Roth IRA. Conversions should be accomplished by December 31 of the student's junior year of high school so as not to impact the FAFSA. You will pay taxes on the converted amount, but you gain the benefit of no future forced withdrawals during the base years. You will have reduced your future income for EFC calculations. Any taxes paid might outweigh the increased aid received. Plus, your Roth IRA can now pass tax-free to a spouse and the tax-free growth stretched even more if passed to children.

As mentioned, the Regular EFC Worksheet includes contributions, adding them in under untaxed income, so contributions do not lower the current year EFC. In fact, a deductible IRA lowers your taxes, which will increase your EFC. The income tax you paid *is used* in calculating your EFC.

This might be a reason to choose a Roth IRA or to make a nondeductible Traditional IRA contribution (skipping the tax deduction entirely). This later option is usually chosen by families whose income falls above the IRA income contribution thresholds.

Roth IRA

The Roth IRA provides greater flexibility and access to your funds. There are no RMDs for the original owner or spouse who inherits the account, and after age 59½ distributions are tax-free. Since you are not forced to take distributions, you have more control.

Modified AGI (MAGI) Limit: To make a 2013 contribution, married filing jointly (MJF) returns must be less than $188,000. Single, head of household, or married filing separately (where you did not live with your spouse at any time during the year) must be less than $127,000.

Roths have the same EFC *asset* protection as a Traditional IRA, but since Roth contributions are not deducted on your taxes, the contributions (not the growth) can be withdrawn at *anytime* for *any purpose* (*See* Example p. 62). Like the Traditional IRA, distributions still count as income for Regular EFC calculations, but distributions are allocated as contributions first, so you pay no taxes.

If you withdraw all your contributions and have to withdraw earnings, the first $10,000 of your earnings will fall under the educational expense exception rule, and no penalty will be owed.

A final big advantage of the Roth is its ability to pass to your heirs where it can continue to grow tax-free. Your Roth IRA can pass to your spouse with no RMDs, and then pass on again to your children with RMDs, all the while, continuing to grow tax-free. This transfer of potential growth is often called "stretching" your IRA and more details can be found in *Parlay Your IRA into a Family Fortune* by Ed Slott.

Student Roth IRAs

Students usually choose a Roth IRA when their income isn't high enough to benefit from the tax deduction connected to the Traditional IRA, or when they just want flexibility and access to their money. The IRA will shield student assets.

> *Example:* Two students each earned $2,000 through part-time employment. The first student saved in a bank, while the second student saved in a Roth IRA. All other factors were the same. The first student will be expected to use $400 (20 percent of assets) to contribute toward paying college costs. The second student has an excluded asset, thus a student asset contribution of zero, and will receive more aid.

Suppose the first student spent all her money, instead of saving in a bank. If her parents wanted more ways to shield their own assets (parent assets), they could contribute to a Roth IRA for the student. The contribution would be limited to the student's earned income or the yearly limit ($5,500 in 2013), whichever is less. In this example, they could contribute $2,000. (If the student had earned $6,000, then $5,500 would be the contribution limit.)

By funding a student Roth IRA, this family shields more money from the EFC calculations. Uncle Sam does not care who funds the Roth IRA as long as neither the earned income amount or yearly contribution limit are exceeded. Grandparents, other relatives, or even friends could fund the Roth IRA of a working student. This is an excellent idea for birthday or Christmas gifts for working students, but you can't "gift" an IRA for a *nonworking* student. The student must have earned income to contribute to an IRA.

IRAs can also be used as incentives for students to work. Parents might offer that for every dollar earned, the parents would contribute a dollar to a Roth IRA in the student's name, similar to an employer matching retirement plan.

Parents should realize they are giving up control of these funds, but the true cost to the parent is technically less than the actual contribution amount. If the parent had not shielded this money, some of it would be tapped for the family EFC anyway.

Some ways students obtain the required earned income are:

1. Students, upon reaching the legal working age (generally age 14 but there are some exceptions), obtain some sort of employment.

2. Students can work in the family business at any age.

3. Students of any age can begin their own business as a sole proprietor and not be subject to the U.S. child labor laws, not subject to the age 14 restriction.

4. Students of any age can become a household employee for the parent. This requires money, time, and commitment on the part of the parent.

Further information on starting Roth IRAs for children can be found in *The Kid's Roth IRA Handbook*, sold online at Amazon.com.

Consider a family with four students earning income. This family can possibly shelter $22,000 ($5,500 x 4 children) *per year* in a Roth IRA.

Even lower contribution amounts add up over time. A family that pays $500 a year to their student household employee from age 5 through 18 will have shielded $6,500 ($500 × 13 years) from the financial aid process. Do this for four children and $26,000 ($6,500 × 4 children) is shielded, and this figure does not even include the potential tax-free growth of the account.

Generally, the goal is to keep assets attributable to the parents because the parents' are assessed at a lower percentage rate, but when you can create income for the student, which becomes invested in a Roth IRA, you totally eliminate the asset from the EFC. IRAs can be used to shift assets into earned income, which is fed into an IRA, eliminating the figure entirely from the EFC.

Concerns about student income begin in spring of junior year of high school. From that point forward, earned income *above* the students Total Allowances is assessed at fifty percent for the EFC (*See* line 41 p. 44). Hours might be reduced, but quitting work as a strategy to gain more aid does not always work (*See* p. 137).

IRA Distribution Jeopardy — Hands Off Your IRA!

The importance of distributions is worth repeating. If you decide (or are required because of your age) to take IRA distributions, the taxable amount (if any) will increase your AGI (appearing on line 15b of the Form 1040). AGI is important to qualify for the Automatic Zero EFC or Simplified Needs Test (SNT), but even if you aren't near those income levels, distributions still increase income for the Regular EFC Worksheet, which means less aid. If you have a choice, take distributions after junior year of college, after signing the last FAFSA, so they are not included in income.

The nontaxable portion of a distribution (which may be original contributions in the case of a Roth IRA) *is also included* in the EFC calculations. It's added back to your AGI for aid determination.

Pulling money from IRAs for educational expenses results in no tax benefits, no financial aid benefits, and a decrease in your financial stability come retirement time. Withdrawing IRA money is simply not the wisest move to make.

IRA and Retirement Plan Rollovers

IRA rollovers should have no impact on your tax return or financial aid. A rollover occurs when you move money from one IRA account to another of the *same* type. The best way to do this is for one institution to transfer (send) the funds to the other, so you never handle the funds yourself.

If you complete a rollover during the base years, do not include this amount on the FAFSA and check that your college does not treat the rollover as a distribution. The rollover appears on the tax form (line 15a of the Form 1040), on the same line as a nontaxable distribution (which would be included as income), so it's fairly easy to make a mistake and categorize a rollover as income.

Schedule Contributions to Raise Your Taxes

If you are not aiming to receive the Automatic Zero EFC or SNT, you probably *do not* want to use a deductible or tax deferment retirement plan. These plans lower your taxes. If you are not trying to meet the income thresholds for the special EFC categories, then *you want your taxes to be high* during base years. Income taxes paid are one of the allowances subtracted out for your EFC calculation (*See* p. 38). The higher your taxes, the lower your EFC will be.

You may have to educate your tax preparer on this fact, or if you use tax software, be aware most software programs aim to reduce your taxes paid. Tax preparers and software programs are not working in the best interest of financial aid.

To keep your taxes high during the base years, you might choose to contribute to a non-deductible traditional IRA or a Roth IRA (which isn't deducted).

When funds are limited choose a Roth IRA or use a deductible plan with contributions grouped to fall in non-base years.

> *Example:* Justin contributes to his employer matching plan to the maximum amount the employer will match. After that, Justin can afford to add $1,000 to an IRA every year ($6,000 over six years). Some options for Justin are illustrated in the table below:

Options:	1) Worst	2) Better	3) Best
IRA Type:	Traditional	Traditional	Roth or non-deductible Traditional IRA
Non-base year (High school sophomore spring semester through fall of junior year)	$1,000	$3,000	$1,000
base year 1	$1,000	0	$1,000
base year 2	$1,000	0	$1,000
base year 3	$1,000	0	$1,000
base year 4	$1,000	0	$1,000
Non-base year	$1,000	$3,000	$1,000
Total Contributed	$6,000	$6,000	$6,000

The worst option for Justin would be the $1,000 contribution to a Traditional IRA (column 1) because this will lower his taxes for every base year. The second option (column 2) will not affect base years, but Justin would have to be able to afford the up-front $3,000 contribution the first year, and as he saves for the second $3,000 contribution, these savings will be assessed as assets, included in the EFC formula. The Roth IRA or a non-deductible Traditional IRA (column 3) appears to be the best choice; it's affordable and does not reduce taxes. Higher taxes helps lower the EFC.

Whole Life Insurance Benefits

The cash value or equity of a life insurance policy isn't included as an asset in the Expected Family Contribution (EFC) formula. A death benefit from a life insurance policy would be reported as untaxed income (money received).

Detailed and consolidated information is not readily available discussing how life insurance can be used for college expenses, so this book devotes a few pages to the subject and includes some of the general benefits of life insurance as well.

Life insurance is not often discussed and analyzed like IRAs. Generally, no one says, "Hey, that's a great decision!" when you announce you've purchased life insurance. It's much more like a car purchase. You may always have a nagging feeling, wondering if you made a smart decision, if you over or under purchased, or if you received the best deal.

Life insurance policies can also be purchased insuring children. Depending on the age of the child, the application might require the child's signatures and medical tests.

There are many types of life insurance (term, universal life, variable life, and whole life) and each type can have numerous variations in policy terms. Policies vary depending on one's age, sex, health, and the amount of death benefit. Because policies can be customized to fit individual needs, it's almost impossible to describe any policy as the "best" deal.

The following discussion is for a whole life policy (dividend paying) at a participating mutual company. It can be compared to alternative plans with an agent if desired. The discussion provides an overview (including college and beyond) of why some parents choose to add a life insurance account to their financial portfolio.

Term Life Insurance

In Term Life Insurance, the policy owner pays a premium that covers a period of time, during which if the insured member dies, a death benefit is paid. There is no cash build up and this type of policy provides no strategy approach for financial aid.

Term Life Insurance

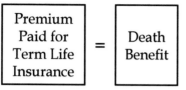

Example of Annual Term Insurance: Dad owns a policy where he is insured and Mom is the beneficiary. He pays an annual premium in January. If he dies at any time during the year, Mom will receive the death benefit. He must pay the premium again every January to be covered for the next year. If he does not renew the policy, the contract is over and no cash is received.

Whole Life Insurance

Whole life insurance includes a cash surrender value as well as a death benefit.

Whole Life Insurance

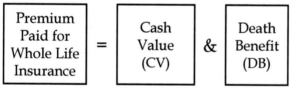

If the owner dies a death benefit is paid. If the owner chooses to close the policy, the cash value is surrendered to the owner.

Policies can also include (earn) dividends. A policy owner can:

1. Receive dividends in cash,

2. Use dividends to purchase additional life insurance, or

3. Use dividends to reduce premiums.

When dividends are received in cash, they are tax-free because they are viewed as a return of premium, not a gain on investment. They do not affect a tax return.

Policies can also include a "waiver of premium" which means the premium will be paid for the owner if the owner ever becomes disabled and cannot work. The extra cost is usually minimal.

Policies can also include riders. A rider means, in addition to purchasing life insurance, the owner pays an additional amount, usually called Additional Paid-Up Insurance (API) or Paid-Up Additions (PUAs). Both APIs and PUAs, hereafter referred to as riders, result in an increase in both cash value and death benefit.

Whole Life Insurance with a Rider and Dividends

Premium Paid for Whole Life Insurance	+	Rider & Dividends	=	Cash Value (CV) + Additional Cash Value for each rider purchased	&	Original Death Benefit (DB) + Additional death benefit with each rider purchased

When the policy isn't cancelled and the insured member dies, the beneficiary receives the original death benefit, plus all the additional death benefit purchased by riders and dividends. The owner never receives both the cash value and the death benefit, and the same is true for the beneficiary. This is why the diagram shows the "&" sign, not a plus sign, for the two components of the account. *You can receive cash value or a death benefit, but not both.*

Money can be pulled from a policy by surrendering riders or taking loans (discussed later). If you withdrew the actual cash value including any dividend additions, the policy would close. This is why it's called the cash *surrender* value. You surrender the policy if the cash is removed.

> *Example of Whole Life Insurance:* A whole life dividend bearing policy at a participating mutual company pays a $250,000 death benefit. Riders are added increasing the death benefit. If the insured member pays up-front annually and dies only one day after signing the policy, the death benefit will pay $250,000 plus any additional insurance purchased by riders. If the insured member dies several years later, the death benefit will have grown, perhaps to $350,000. The cash value will also have grown. This cash value allows the owner to take loans. This cash value is also the amount surrendered if the policy was ever cancelled.

Whole life is useful when planning financially because it builds cash. Cash removed from the policy through loans, dividends or surrendering riders can be used at the owner's wish. There are no restrictions. Some people save in whole life plans for retirement.

Because the cash value of life insurance is not an asset for the EFC formula, these policies can also be established to shield parent and student assets, as well as a possible source for loans.

The following list includes common reason people purchase whole life insurance. The first two heavily impact college.

Reasons for purchasing whole life insurance:

1. To shield assets from federal financial aid computations

2. To act as a place to take a college loan

3. To take a loan without having to justify its use

4. To take a loan without credit checks

5. To have the power to repay a loan at the policy owner's terms (including skipping payments and the option to never repay the loan)

6. To save at a safe fixed guaranteed rate

7. To earn tax-free or tax-deferred dividends

8. To use money without age restrictions or penalties

9. To establish an emergency fund immune to the economy

10. To eliminate future life insurance denial for a child

11. To insure a child for the purpose of wealth growth

12. To cover the costs of closing one's estate

13. To provide financial security for one's heirs

14. To provide for a child support requirement in cases of divorce or separation

15. To pass on an IRA untouched to heirs

16. To possibly exclude assets subject to lawsuit

Each of these is explained next.

To shield assets from federal aid computations

Cash owned in a life insurance policy is not counted as an asset when computing financial aid.

If you learn about life insurance shortly before completing the FAFSA, it may not be too late to make a financial impact on your EFC. You can consider backdating a life insurance policy or loading it initially with a large sum of cash. Both strategies will quickly move funds out of the asset category for EFC calculations.

Before you open a policy for the purpose of shielding assets, first find out if you even need to shield your assets. Students who qualify for either the Automatic Zero EFC or the Simplified Needs Test will not use assets in their EFC calculations, so they have no reason to be concerned with shielding them.

Even if assets will not be used to calculate your EFC, you might still consider life insurance for one of the other listed reasons.

To act as a place to take a college loan

As the cash value of a whole life insurance policy builds, the policy can eventually be used as a loan source. The loan could be for a car, a down payment on a home, a vacation, or a loan for college. Life insurance has similarities to a savings account; however, when you withdraw money from a savings account, the money no longer earns interest. When you take a loan from a whole life insurance policy, the account continues to earn the guaranteed rate plus dividends on the original balance.

> *Example:* Family A has saved $30,000 in their savings account which earns interest. Family A removes $10,000 for college and it now has $20,000 in the savings account earning interest.

> Family B has a life insurance policy on Dad that earns interest plus dividends and has grown to $30,000 in cash value. Family B removes $10,000 for college. It now has $30,000 earning interest and dividends, plus a loan debt of $10,000. The cash value balance does not reduce to $20,000.

Before the loan, Family B has

Cash Value $30,000	&	Original Death Benefit + Additional Death Benefits

After the loan, Family B has

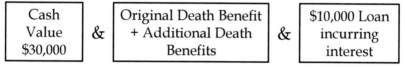

Cash Value $30,000	&	Original Death Benefit + Additional Death Benefits	&	$10,000 Loan incurring interest

Family B earns interest and dividends on the original $30,000 even though it appears they removed $10,000. This happens because Family B never touched the $30,000. The $30,000 is acting as collateral for the existing loan.

Of course, Family B did not obtain $10,000 for free. The cost for Family B is the interest paid on the $10,000 loan. Family A also has a cost involved. Family A loses the interest they would have earned on the $10,000 removed from the savings account.

With a participating policy at a mutual insurance company, the policy owner is legally considered an owner in the company and because of this, shares in company profits. As the company profits off the interest paid by Family B, higher dividends should be paid to all policy owners. All policy holders share in the interest Dad pays, but Dad also shares in the interest other policy owners pay. Dad could view this as if he is *paying some interest back to himself.*

Family B will want to pay the interest on a yearly basis so it does not compound. One of the biggest criticisms of life insurance loans surrounds the fear that owners will be undisciplined and never repay the loan plus interest. Compounding loan interest can eventually reduce the life insurance death benefit itself because when the owner passes away, the company pays the death benefit less the outstanding loan balance, including the outstanding interest.

To take a loan without having to justify its use

Most lenders require you to explain what a loan will be used for (to buy a car, buy a house, fund college, etc.). Life insurance loans can also be used for these items, but the company requires no knowledge of how the loan will be used; no questions are asked.

To take a loan without credit checks

When you take a loan from your life insurance policy, there is no credit check reflecting how you've handled finances in the past, no one to say your loan is denied, and no one asking how you plan to repay this loan. It doesn't matter what your credit rating is, you automatically have the power to take the loan.

To repay a loan at the policy owner's terms

When you take a loan from your life insurance policy, you have the power to decide when to pay it back and how often to make repayments. You can begin immediately, skip payments, or delay repayment for a number of years. Because of this control, a life insurance loan might be a good source for a college loan.

After taking a loan, Family B, in the example, has two options:

1. *Repay the loan*

   If Family B repays the loan, as the policy owner, Family B decides the monetary amount and increments for repayment. Family B could pay only the yearly interest until after graduation, or decide to begin immediate monthly repayments. If a medical emergency should happen, repayments could be temporarily ceased.

2. *Never Repay the Loan*

   If Family B never repays the loan, either:

   a. A surrendered policy will receive a reduced cash value, or

   b. With the policy in place, the owner continues to receive dividends either directly or reinvested in the policy, and upon death, a reduced death benefit is received, or

   c. Dividends can be used to repay the loan

   Note: Annual interest should always be paid, even if the plan is to never repay the loan.

Recall, the life insurance account for Family B looks like this:

Cash Value $30,000	&	Original Death Benefit + Additional Death Benefits	&	$10,000 Loan incurring interest

An account is closed by either calling the company to close it or by the insured member's death. For Family B, closing the account could be illustrated by the diagram below. The cash value would be reduced by $10,000 or the death benefit would be reduced by $10,000, as shown:

Call and close		Close because of member's death
$30,000 Cash Value −$10,000 Loan $20,000 Cash Surrender Value	or	Original Death Benefit + Additional Death Benefit (DB) − $10,000 loan purchased Actual Death Benefit (reduced)

Cash Surrender Value: If Dad lives and decides to never repay the loan, at any time the family could cash out the policy (close it) and receive the $20,000 in cash surrender value.

Pay Death Benefit: If Dad should pass away the day after obtaining the loan, Family B never has to worry about the loan (because the loan is automatically paid off) and the family will receive a reduced death benefit to handle family affairs.

In most cases, the reduced death benefit will never be less than the original death benefit purchased (because the rider continues to purchase more death benefit). It is possible though, for unpaid interest to compound on an unpaid loan and eventually begin to reduce the original death benefit amount.

Interest rates are set in the policy contract. Rates can be fixed or variable, fluctuating with current rates.

Interest should always be paid to ensure the original death benefit amount will remain in place to provide for heirs (which is the typical intention of purchasing life insurance to begin with).

Whole Life Insurance Illustration, 15 year old female

Year	Age	Annual Premium	Guaranteed Cash Value	Non-guaranteed Cash Value
1	15	2,180	826	826
2	16	2,180	2,708	2,777
3	17	2,180	4,663	4,839
4	18	2,180	6,695	7,024
5	19	2,180	8,803	9,339
6	20	2,180	10,995	11,882
7	21	2,180	13,275	14,668
8	22	2,180	15,642	17,708
9	23	2,180	18,106	21,020
10	24	2,180	20,666	24,532
11	**25**	**0**	**21,416**	**25,915**
12	26	0	22,195	27,385
13	27	0	22,999	28,938
14	28	0	23,832	30,591
15	29	0	24,695	32,345
16	30	0	25,590	34,211
17	31	0	26,514	36,185
18	32	0	27,472	38,278
19	33	0	28,461	40,493
20	34	0	29,483	42,837
21	35	0	30,534	45,315
22	36	0	31,622	47,940
23	37	0	32,743	50,713
24	38	0	33,904	53,654
25	39	0	35,104	56,770
26	40	0	36,344	60,067
27	41	0	37,627	63,562
28	42	0	38,950	67,258
29	43	0	40,315	71,171
30	**44**	**0**	**41,720**	**75,305**

Recover Cost Basis ——→ (Year 11)

3.53 % Rate of Return ——→ (Year 30)

6.10 % Rate of Return

To save at a safe fixed guaranteed rate

Life insurance should not be thought of as a compounding growth investment. It's comparable to safe entities like savings accounts, Certificates of Deposit (CDs), annuities, and bonds with the big difference being, life insurance also comes with a death benefit. It's a good foundation element for any investment plan.

Whole life insurance plans include a guaranteed interest rate. Because of fees involved, for the cash value to actually show this rate, the owner must hold the plan in place for many years. The first years have negative growth, but this growth continually increases until it reaches or surpasses the guaranteed rate. This concept of *hold for a guaranteed rate* is similar to CDs.

Looking at an illustration, you can determine when you are guaranteed to recover your cost basis and the rates of return.

> *Example:* Part of a policy illustration for a fifteen year old female with a guaranteed rate of 4 percent is shown on the opposite page. This policy is called a 10-pay, which means the owner pays premiums *for only ten years,* but the death benefit is *good for the life* of the insured member. After ten years, the cost basis is $21,800 ($2,180 annual premium × 10 years).

> In the illustration, the basis of $21,800 is almost recovered by year 11, when the guaranteed cash value is $21,416.

> An annual return calculator for a portfolio is found at http://www.mymoneyblog.com/estimate-your-portfolios-rate-of-return-calculator.html.

> Using this *rough estimate* calculator, when $21,800 has been invested for 30 years and cash value is $41,720, the rate of return calculates to 3.53 percent (not yet 4 percent).

After thirty years, the account is acting like it earned 3.53 percent *every year* since year inception (not the guaranteed 4 percent). It's slow steady growth, not to be compared to stocks. (The nonguaranteed column is a *guess* at how the cash value will look with dividends, in this case $75,305, for a 6.1 percent rate of return, which exceeds the guaranteed 4 percent.)

The death benefit (not shown) began at $150,000, and after 30 years was $158,777 guaranteed, and $281,954 nonguaranteed.

To earn tax-free or tax-deferred dividends

Annual dividends can be withdrawn or left within the policy to purchase more insurance, a greater death benefit.

As long as dividends withdrawn do not exceed premiums paid, they will be considered a return of premium and be tax-free with no impact on a tax return and thus, no impact on your EFC.

Recall, the *after-tax rate* is a term referring to the rate your investment earned once taxes are factored in *(See* p. 66). In this case, since no gain is reported for tax purposes, the after-tax rate is always equal to or better than the guaranteed rate of the policy.

Once dividends withdrawn exceed the total premiums paid, the excess becomes taxable. Dividends that exceed premiums are tax-deferred. This means you didn't pay taxes on them when declared, but instead paid taxes on them later, when withdrawn.

Keeping gains off your tax return is always desirable, but avoiding dividends can impact other areas as well. The following example shows how avoiding dividends with life insurance helps a lower income single parent.

> *Example:* In 2013, single mom Sue, with three children, raises her children on child support received and her earnings of about $16,000 a year.
>
> Sue would like to qualify for the 2013 Earned Income Credit (EIC), a refundable credit worth up to $6,044. To qualify, Sue's 2013 *investment income* must be under $3,300. Unfortunately, Sue's dividend stocks and capital gains from mutual funds are projected to earn roughly $3,500 in investment income. This income is undesirable because it both disqualifies Sue for EIC and increases her EFC, reducing the student aid received.
>
> Sue decides to reduce her reported investment income by selling her dividend bearing stocks, and instead, purchasing a dividend paying whole life policy. By eliminating dividends from her tax return, she qualifies for EIC, increases her refund by $6,044, and she might save this extra money to pay for college.

If you thought dividend bearing life insurance was only for the wealthy, Sue's example demonstrates how it can be used to assist lower income families as well.

To use money without age restrictions or penalties

Funds may be removed from life insurance policies by taking loans, receiving dividends, or surrendering riders. The technicalities of how this is accomplished will be explained by your agent.

What's important to note here is there are no penalties when removing funds. Other accounts like Certificates of Deposit (CDs) or retirement funds usually incur penalties and lose interest if one decides to remove money early.

There are also no age restrictions attached with life insurance. Accounts like Traditional Individual Retirement Accounts (IRAs) require investors to wait until a certain age for withdrawals.

To establish an emergency fund immune to the economy

Life insurance can be used as a place for a safe secure emergency fund to cover living expenses from three months to a year or more. Funds can be removed without concern of the current economy, stock market conditions, or how the money will affect a tax return. There is no timing pressure to sell when the market is high, and usually the transaction does not impact a tax return.

To eliminate future life insurance denial for a child

By insuring children, you can be sure they will never be denied life insurance. Perhaps the family's medical history causes concern of future approval or perhaps parents just wish to protect any chance of the unknown (such as being diagnosed with diabetes or HIV/AIDS). Parents could purchase life insurance on their child and later pass ownership of this policy to the child.

To insure a child for the purpose of wealth growth

When parents insure their children, these policies also grow in cash value, at guaranteed rates, earning dividends, with the same loan benefits. Upon the parents' death, ownership transfers automatically to the child and if the parent wishes to pass the policy on sooner, it can be gifted to the child, who can then use it to take loans and provide security for heirs.

To cover the costs of closing one's estate

A person with no dependents could purchase life insurance for the sole purpose of handling his or her estate. Someone has to complete paperwork, pay off any debts, perhaps sell the home, etc. All this requires time and perhaps hiring persons of expertise. Life insurance will help cover all the costs involved.

To provide financial security for one's heirs

The most common reason to purchase life insurance is to provide for heirs. Life insurance ensures financial support for the family to live and perhaps enough to go to college.

To provide for a child support requirement

Life insurance is often connected to child support in cases of separating or divorcing parents. Usually the noncustodial parent must maintain life insurance to ensure the support obligation will be paid even in the event of death. In such cases a whole life plan with a mutual insurance company, building cash and dividends might be considered, especially for the college benefits.

Often divorce decrees require only the noncustodial parent to maintain life insurance. In reality child support is a joint obligation, so it could be argued for both parents to maintain life insurance payable to the opposite party in the case of one's death. The required amount of insurance should be proportional to the percentages assigned each parent by state support laws.

> *Example:* Jim and custodial parent, Amy, have a combined child support amount of $1,000 divided 75/25. It might be ordered for Jim to obtain life insurance for 75 percent of the total obligation, and Amy to maintain life insurance for the remaining 25 percent, with each opposing party listed as the beneficiary. This ensures, should Amy pass away, Jim would not be 25 percent short, and vise versa.

Usually the insurance amount needed is until the child turns age 18 or 21. Parents could agree to above and beyond this amount, agreeing to maintain enough to cover for college expenses.

To pass on an IRA untouched to heirs

Life insurance makes other investments work better by providing flexibility. If you have both life insurance and an Individual Retirement Account (IRA), you might advise your heirs on which to spend first. Since the death benefit is a lump sum, no longer growing with tax benefits, usually it should be spent first.

Life insurance can be used to handle estate expenses and then, the IRA will pass untouched to heirs, continuing to grow (tax-free if it's a Roth or tax-deferred if it's a Traditional IRA).

> *Example:* A Roth IRA can pass to your spouse with no required distributions, and then pass on again to your children with required distributions, all the while, continuing to grow tax-free. This transfer of potential growth is often called "stretching" your IRA.

To exclude assets subject to lawsuits

While you hope to never be involved in a lawsuit, it can happen. In some states, the cash value of life insurance is a protected asset and cannot be seized. This fact might be extremely significant to a family which owns a business, where the chance of being sued is certainly higher than a family with no business asset. In the case of some unforeseen future liability, this family could rest a little easier knowing at least some of their family assets were protected and these protected funds could be used for college.

Child Policies

Depending on the child's age, applications for insuring a child sometimes require medical tests and the child's signature. To avoid repeating a test, athletes should not provide urine samples within four hours of physical exercise as this may skew the numbers and require the test to be repeated.

Making the Decision on Life Insurance

With all the positive reasons to consider purchasing life insurance, should you rush out to buy policies on every family member?

Life insurance adds diversity and balance to a financial portfolio. It's often used to replace the bond portion of a portfolio, providing safe slow guaranteed growth while reducing volatility.

Begin by reviewing the list (*See* p. 81) and checking off the reasons that appeal to you. If the FAFSA rules change, or if the tax treatment changes, would you still want to own a policy?

If you are still interested, you might consult several agents and compare different mutual companies. The benefits discussed here apply to a whole life dividend paying participating (meaning that company gains are shared amongst policy owners) policy at a mutual company, preferably one in existence for many years.

If your goal is to shelter cash, you might ask your agent about backdating a policy or if there are options to load the policy at the start. The partial illustration for a student policy (*See* p. 86) was at a conservative premium of $2,180 a year or $181.67 per month. You could open a policy for less, maybe a $100 each month, or open a policy for $1,000 or more a month, if you have the funds.

Many of the benefits of life insurance can be found elsewhere. There are other ways to provide for heirs, create emergency funds, and shield assets from the EFC formula. There are several ways to achieve the numerous life insurance benefits previously listed.

Consider the following families with a $10,000 college bill:

1. *Savings Account Method:* A person removes $10,000 from a savings account earning five percent interest. At the end of the year, this person has spent $10,000 and lost $500 in interest. This is a Lost Opportunity Cost (LOC). (The interest that would have been earned in the savings account has been lost.) The total cost is $10,500.

2. *Loan Method:* A person takes a $10,000 loan at five percent interest. At the end of the year, this person has spent $10,000 and paid $500 in interest. The total cost is $10,500.

3. *Life Insurance Method:* A person takes a $10,000 insurance loan at five percent interest against the cash value of a policy. This person pays the $500 interest back to the company. At the end of the year, this person has spent $10,000 and paid $500 in interest. The total cost is $10,500.

In each case, $10,000 is spent and $500 is given up as interest or a loss of investment (a Lost Opportunity Cost). When the rates are the same, the only real difference is the method chosen. In the first case, the money is saved first and spent later, commonly referred to as *Save and Spend*. In the second case, the money is borrowed, and the third case is really another version of *Save and Spend* because money must be saved in the life insurance policy prior to taking a loan. The end result is everyone's cost is $10,500.

The term "recapture" is often mentioned when discussing life insurance loans. Recapture refers to capturing the original cost of your purchase plus interest, as if you never paid anything at all. In all three cases, you are really *saving again* to bring yourself back to your original position. Assume each person repays in a year:

1. *Savings Account Method:* The person who withdrew $10,000 from savings treats this account like a bank and treats the withdrawal as a loan. He repays the account with five percent interest (just like a loan). (The assumption is this person is disciplined enough to do this.) Upon repayment, this person has $10,500 (exactly what would have occurred if there had been no withdrawal). Some would call this recaptured. Some would say this person just saved again.

2. *Loan Method:* The person who took a $10,000 loan pays the loan off plus $500 in interest, and thus has not "recaptured" anything but is in fact also in the original position. This person began with no cash, spent $10,500, and ended with no cash.

3. *Life Insurance Method:* The person, who took a loan of $10,000 against the cash value of a life insurance account, repays the insurance company at five percent interest. The company receives $500 and $10,000 is no longer held against the cash value. This person spent $10,500 and saved again to end up in the original position.

The net result at this point is the same. Each person has returned to the original position with the same amount spent. No one really recaptured anything, but instead saved again. The point is, if you have life insurance *and all rates are equal*, it would not matter whether you removed $10,000 from an insurance policy, $10,000 from your savings, or took a $10,000 loan. Of course, *rates will not be equal*, so usually, you would choose the lowest rate.

When other factors like credit rating, repayment schedules, or the ability to skip payments are important, then you might choose to borrow from a life insurance policy, even if it has a higher rate.

In presenting any argument pro or con, the economy (the real world) matters. Often savings accounts earn between one and two percent interest (not the five percent illustrated above). Loan interest is low today, but will rise in the future and loans are harder to obtain today than they were five years ago. All these factors will influence your life insurance decision.

Sometimes the third person, the whole life policy owner, finds the cash value has increased. For example, instead of $10,500, this person has $10,600. This gain happens in participating insurance companies that pay dividends on the full cash value—as if there was no loan against it. The policy owner shares in the interest paid to the company. In this example, the owner gained $100 as a result of sharing in the company gains, receiving company dividends. This could be viewed as the owner recapturing interest or *paying yourself back*, but since dividends are not guaranteed, policy owners cannot claim they will always come out ahead of the other scenarios.

Policy owners can claim, they did the same as the others, but with a bonus—the death benefit.

A second critical difference, relevant to the focus of this book, is in the first scenario, the $10,000 in savings, earns taxable interest and is also an asset when computing the EFC (unless the person qualified for an Automatic Zero or the Simplified Needs Test). This is another example of how the EFC formula penalizes those who save. The key is to save in things that are not declared assets.

Two factors of whole life insurance that cannot be argued are:

1. Whole life insurance grows risk free at a fixed guaranteed rate along with a death benefit and

2. There is no other place to have the flexibility to take a loan with the same terms

> *Example:* Try asking a lending institution, "Could you not run a credit check, but provide me with a loan (regardless of my age), with no penalty should I ever miss a re-payment, no scheduled repayments (actually, I may not pay it back at all), and by the way, I'm not going to tell you what this loan will be used for."

The main flaw with life insurance is there is a risk at getting behind in premium payments and a risk that owners will not repay their loans, including interest, which in the long run reduces the death benefit. This should be addressed at the time of purchase with a good evaluation of one's budget.

After as certain number of years, a policy can pay for itself by using annual dividends or surrendering riders or dividends. When purchasing a policy, you should understand when this will happen. You should be able to pay premiums through that year without running into financial difficulty.

Life insurance agents should help with this financial planning, estimating your budget and future financial needs, to arrive at a reasonable figure for both the premiums and the death benefit.

To find the cash to pay for a life insurance policy, review options with an agent. Perhaps there is money in your tax refund, your current savings account, or your emergency fund. Perhaps you could eliminate a nonessential monthly expense such as cable TV. Perhaps you have a bonus or were already considering getting a second job to begin saving for college. How about stopping non-matching contributions to an employer plan? A good experienced agent will shed ideas that you may not think of.

Should you purchase life insurance before funding other investments, like an IRA? If funding life insurance makes you eligible for $5,666 in Earned Income Credit (as in our example on p. 88) or you need it to provide security for your heirs, then perhaps life insurance should come first. If you want to transfer tax-free wealth to heirs that will continue growing tax-free, perhaps a Roth IRA should come first. If your company has a matching retirement plan, where they will match deposits you make, that is also a worthwhile investment. Perhaps, for a balanced portfolio, you would save in all three places. There is no right answer that applies to everyone.

Life insurance is an option for parents and students to explore to possibly add diversity to an investment portfolio while shielding assets from the financial aid calculations. This is a strategy that can be started with a newborn or used the year you sign the FAFSA application (using additional techniques such as back-dating policies and front loading). All of the possible strategies in this book require further educated advice based on personal circumstances. The next page has a list of questions to help you in discussions with life insurance agents.

Questions to discuss with a life insurance agent

1. How much insurance does my family of (#) persons need?

2. Will you review my income and expenses and suggest ways I can comfortable afford this policy?

3. Should I save in life insurance before my IRA or employer matching plan?

4. Is your company a mutual company that pays dividends?

5. Is this policy a Direct Recognition or Non-direct Recognition and could you explain the terms?

6. Is this a participating or non-participating company?

7. Should I pay premiums annually or monthly and why?

8. At what year will I recover my cost basis?

9. At what year can the policy pay for itself?

10. At what year will the policy be paid in full?

11. What is the guaranteed interest rate and the loan rate?

12. Using the cost basis in the computation, when does my policy reflect the guaranteed rate? (*See* example p. 81)

13. Is my money FDIC insured?

14. How long has your company been in business and how does your company rate when compared to others? Ratings are found at:

    * A.M. Best - http://www.ambest.com
    * Fitch Ratings - http://www.fitchratings.com
    * Moody's Investors Services - http://www.moodys.com
    * Standard & Poor's - http://www.standardandpoors.com

15. What happens if the company declares bankruptcy?

16. Is this a protected asset (off limits) if I were to be sued?

17. Will I always speak to you every time I call?

18. What happens if you pass away before I do?

19. Who handles the paperwork (death certificate, pension forms, IRAs, social security, etc.) for my beneficiaries?

U.S. Series EE/I Savings Bonds

U.S. Series EE/I Savings bonds are another type of investment. They do not fall in the excluded asset category, but they are an investment with potential educational benefits.

EE and I bonds usually grow tax-deferred, meaning the interest isn't declared on one's taxes until the bond is cashed. (Sometimes owners choose to declare the interest on an annual basis but this decision must be made in the first year and it's uncommon.)

These bonds have an education tax exclusion, permitting all or part of the interest to be declared tax-free. Some advantages are:

1. They are a safe place to save for retirement, an emergency, or other contingencies.

2. When cashed, they are free from state and local taxes.

3. Funds are not restricted only for college use.

4. They have guaranteed steady (not aggressive) growth.

5. They have an education tax exclusion.

6. If purchased before marriage, some states consider EE/I Bonds to be *separate property*, belonging solely to the owner; not to be divided in cases of divorce.

Bonds will be an *asset of the owner* until cashed in, at which time the growth will be *income for the owner*, either taxable or nontaxable depending on their use. Families qualifying for the Simplified Needs Test (SNT) or the Automatic Zero EFC need to be careful that cashing bonds does not raise their AGI on their tax return so high that they are disqualified from these categories. Families might consider cashing bonds prior to the base years to avoid their AGI impact, but these bonds would then lose their favorable tax-exclusion rate because there would be no college expenses.

You must report the *current market value* (your basis plus accumulated interest) on the FAFSA. To value your bond, go online to http://www.treasurydirect.gov/BC/SBCPrice. If you own several bonds, you can download the *free* savings bond wizard online at http://www.treasurydirect.gov/indiv/tools/tools_savingsbondwizard_download.htm. Enter all your bonds and you will have an easy quick method to obtain their total value each year for the FAFSA.

Bonds can be redeemed after twelve months, but they have a 3-month interest penalty if redeemed in the first five years. When you cash a bond, you will have a Lost Opportunity Cost. You lose the interest that bond would have earned. Bonds receive compounded interest semiannually for 30 years.[23]

Bonds should be redeemed after an anniversary date.

> *Example*: A EE Bond has a *next interest date* of 02/2014. If this bond is cashed in January, 2014, the last five months of interest will be lost. It should be cashed in February.

Pro Rata Applied to Bonds

The tax exclusion for bonds requires the entire proceeds (principal and interest) to be used for eligible tuition and fees. When proceeds exceed the education costs, the IRS will apply a pro rata formula.

> *Example:* College expenses are $8,000, so you liquidate $10,000 in EE bonds, thinking the $5,000 interest included will be tax free. You also withdraw $3,000 from a 529 Plan and want those tax-free benefits too. *This will not work.*
>
> The $10,000 bond proceeds exceed the total expenses. The, IRS will apply pro rata rules and declare 80 percent ($8,000 expenses/$10,000 total proceeds) of the interest tax-free. This means $4,000 (80 percent × $5,000 interest) is tax free. You will pay taxes on $1,000 of the interest.[24]
>
> But, if you go that route, you might pay a penalty on the $3,000 withdrawn from the 529 Plan. Instead, you declare $3,000 from the 529 Plan as used for education expenses. This leaves only $5,000 of expenses to apply to the bonds. Now, you must recalculate. Only 50 percent ($5,000 in expenses/$10,000 proceeds) of the interest is tax-free. You will pay taxes on $2,500 of bond interest.

---

23. Treasury Direct, *I and EE Savings Bond Comparison*, http://www. treasurydirect.gov/indiv/research/indepth/ebonds/res_e_bonds_eecomparison.htm

24. Treasury Direct, *Using Savings Bonds for Education*, http://www. treasurydirect.gov/forms/savpdp0051.pdf

Tax Exclusion Conditions

Bonds come with a tax-exclusion option, but to exclude *all* the growth, the *entire proceeds* must be declared against educational expenses (as illustrated in the previous example). To be eligible to exclude *any of the growth*, the following conditions must be met:

1. The bond must be issued (purchased) after 1989.

2. The bond owner must have been at least 24 years of age when the bond was issued (purchased).

   — *Note:* Bonds purchased as gifts for new babies should be issued in the name of a parent over age 24.

3. The bond owner, the owner's spouse, or the owner's dependent has educational expenses (*tuition and fees*, not room and board) at a postsecondary educational institution *in the same year that the bond was cashed.* (Save receipts.)

4. The bond owner's income must be under a threshold based on filing status, and the bond interest *is included* as income for this limit. **Modified AGI (MAGI) Limit:** For 2013, MAGI must be less than $89,700 if single or Head of Household and under $142,050 if Married Filing Jointly or qualifying widow(er) with dependent child.

> **Modified Adjusted Gross Income (MAGI):** is your AGI without items normally subtracted: such as EE/I bond interest, IRAs, student loan interest, Tuition and Fees deductions and several other items. (*See* http://www.IRS.gov for a full definition.)

   Example: Parents with a $138,000 AGI cash $10,000 of EE bonds for college. The parents' MAGI of $143,000 ($138,000 + $5,000 bond growth) exceeds their income limit. The bond growth cannot be declared tax-free.

5. When the bond owner is married, the owner must file a tax return as Married Filing Jointly.

6. The child may not be listed as co-owner of the bond but may be listed as the beneficiary.[25]

---

25. IRS, Form, 8815, Exclusion of Interest From Series EE/I U.S. Savings Bonds Issued After 1989, http://www.irs.gov/pub/irs-pdf/f8815.pdf

Qualified Education Accounts

Qualified Education Accounts are another place to save where your growth is declared tax-free when used for eligible education expenses. You cannot deduct your contributions on your federal taxes, but some states provide credits on their state taxes.

When considering saving in these accounts consider:

1. Ownership (whose asset it will be for EFC calculations)

2. How distributions will affect income in EFC calculations

3. Restrictions or penalties pertaining to the use of the funds or any penalties for early withdrawals

4. How they can't be used for the education tax benefits (education deductions and credits)

No Double Dipping: You can only claim (receive) one tax benefit per expense. Think of this like matching education receipts to tax benefits. If you use $1,000 in expenses (receipts) against your $1,000 education account withdrawal, you now need different expenses (receipts) to claim an education tax benefit (*See also* p. 102 & 118)

For a student reporting parental information, all education savings accounts are reported as parental investments, including all accounts owned by the student and all accounts owned by the parents for *any member* of the household.[26]

Third Party Accounts & Distributions

You might think a good strategy to shield these accounts from EFC calculations would be to have a third party (friends, grandparent, or noncustodial parent) own the account and the student named the beneficiary. This works fine until a withdrawal is made.

A third party account *will* shield the asset, but once a distribution is made, the money received will count as is *untaxed income for the student,* assessed at the student's rate of 50 percent. This distribution affects the current award year if taken before signing the FAFSA, or next year's award if taken after signing.

---

26. 2014-2015 FAFSA Application *Investments Also Include* p. 2, https://fafsa.ed.gov/fotw1415/pdf/PdfFafsa14-15.pdf

When you learn about this rule, there may already be accounts owned by a third party with the student as the beneficiary.
In these cases, you might try one of these two solutions:

1. See if you can change the owner to the parent or

2. Try to wait and take distributions after FAFSA submission in senior year of college, so the income will not affect aid. (This also assumes younger siblings will not be in college.)

Qualified Tuition Programs (QTPs)

College Savings Plans (Section 529 Plans)

College Savings Plans are also called Section 529 plans or State-Sponsored College Savings Plans. They are accounts aimed at saving for college. Because they are included assets, 529 Plans are best for high income families who already have their retirement accounts fully funded and cannot receive need-based aid or claim education tax benefits. Some advantages of 529 Plans are:

1. They are an asset of the owner (parent, relative or student), in the owner's control even after a beneficiary turns age 21.

2. The beneficiary can also be the owner.

3. The beneficiary can be changed to another family member.

    — If your first child receives scholarships or chooses not to attend college, you can switch the beneficiary to pass the funds on to another child.

4. The account grows tax-deferred, and the growth is tax-free when used for qualified higher education expenses at an accredited school in the U.S. (and some foreign schools).

5. Some states offer a state tax deduction for contributions made to a Section 529 plan. (*See also* p. 127)

6. Owners may withdraw the entire account (take the money back) but incur taxes and penalties. (This is advantageous over something like a trust where the custodian no longer owns the money.)

7. Computer technology and equipment, Internet access and related service expenses are now eligible. Room and board must be incurred by students enrolled at least half-time.

Some concerns with these plans are:

1. *Influenced by market highs and lows:* You may need to withdraw funds when share prices are low.

2. *Restricted use:* Section 529 plans have taxes and penalties when the money isn't used for education or if the amount withdrawn exceeds education costs. (What is the plan if your children all receive scholarships?)

3. *No Tax Credits or Deductions:* Expenses cannot be mixed with credits or deductions. If you take the tax-free benefit of a 529 plan for educational expenses, you cannot use the same expenses for an education tax credit or deduction.

If your account is below the basis (lost money) due to the recent market drop, perhaps now is the time to withdrawal the funds and use them for whatever you choose. You would pay no taxes or penalty because there is no growth in the account.

A withdrawal from a 529 plan generates a Form 1099Q, reported to the IRS in the name of either the owner or beneficiary, and will *not* be marked as a qualified distribution. The only way an organization can mark it as a qualified distribution is for you to request the money be sent directly to the college, which you may not wish to do, if you want to use the funds for expenses other than tuition. Distributions used for educational expenses will not affect your AGI; they are not income for the EFC:

"As long as distributions from QTPs and ESAs do not exceed the qualified education expenses for which they are intended, they are tax-free, so they will not appear in the next year's AGI. They should not be treated as untaxed income (except [for third-party ownership distributions]) or as estimated financial assistance."[27]

Prepaid Tuition Plans (Section 529 Plans)

Prepaid Tuition Plans are a type of Section 529 Plan where parents pay tuition at today's rates with the promise that the payment will cover the future cost of tuition, regardless of any increases. As a 529 Plan, they have all the previously discussed advantages and disadvantages, but they are usually much more conservative investments, so you have less risk of losing money.

27. Application and Verification Guide 2013-2014, *Filling out the FAFSA,* "Qualified Education Benefits,", p. 18, http://ifap.ed.gov/fsahandbook/attachments/1314AVG.pdf

Coverdell Education Savings Accounts (ESAs)

Coverdell accounts used to be known as *Educational IRAs* because like IRAs, they have tax-sheltered growth, but they differ in that the contributions are not tax deductible. Similar to U.S. savings bonds, distributions will be tax free to the extent they do not exceed the beneficiary's qualified expenses.

There are no state tax breaks for contributions, but most states treat withdrawals as tax-free if used for education. They follow the same EFC rules as 529 Plans: they are an *asset of the owner* and tax-free (not affecting your AGI) when used for college.

There is an income threshold limit to participate and you have until your tax filing deadline to contribute. The limit for annual contributions remains at $2,000 and grades k-12 eligible expenses qualify.

The student does not necessarily gain access to these accounts at age 18 or 21 (as might happen with a trust). These accounts can remain inaccessible until a student reaches age 30, at which time funds would be paid out to the beneficiary. Unlike 529 Pans, parents cannot change their minds and cash out these accounts. Parents can change beneficiaries at any time to another family member under age 30, so there is some ability to shift, but not take back funds.

Coverdell accounts can also be rolled over (transferred) to other institutions or 529 Plans with the same beneficiary and without incurring any penalty. You also have more control in choosing the type of funds the account is invested in.

Education Accounts and Divorce

In a divorce, educational accounts are usually not divided, but instead, declared *property of the children*. The custodial parent might take ownership of the accounts so the asset will be assessed at this parent's lower rate for the EFC. By avoiding ownership by the noncustodial parent, you avoid future third party distributions counting as income to the student. The decree should grant account inquiry access to the noncustodial parent, and it should also declare a future division of any unused funds, along with their accumulated growth.

Trusts and Custodial Accounts

Trusts accounts managed by a trustee are generally assets of the beneficiary unless access is restricted by a court order. For your convenience, see this from the Application and Verification Guide:

> "Trust funds in the name of a student, spouse, or parent should be reported as that person's asset on the application, generally even if the beneficiary's access to the trust is restricted. If the settlor of a trust has voluntarily placed restrictions on its use, then the student should report its present value as an asset, as discussed below. If a trust has been restricted by court order, however, the student should not report it. An example of such a restricted trust is one set up by court order to pay for future surgery for the victim of a car accident.

> * *Interest only:* Interest paid out from trusts is reported as income for the recipient in the year paid out, otherwise accumulating interest is reported as a current asset.
> * *Principal only:* The person who will receive only the trust principal must report as an asset the present value of his right to that principal.
>   — Example: If a $10,000 principal reverts to a dependent student's parents when the trust ends and the student is receiving the interest, report the interest as student income and report the present value of the trust as a parental asset. (The present value is the amount that a third person would pay for the right to receive the principal 10 years from now—basically, the amount that one would have to deposit now to receive $10,000 in 10 years.)
> * *Both principal and interest:* If a student, spouse, or parent receives both the interest and the principal from the trust, the student should report the present value of both interest and principal, as described in the discussion of principal only. If the trust is set up so that the interest accumulates within the trust until it ends, the beneficiary should report as an asset the

present value of the interest and principal that she is expected to receive when the trust ends.

"The Uniform Gifts and Uniform Transfers to Minors Acts (UGMA and UTMA) allow the establishment of an account for gifts of cash and financial assets for a minor without the expense of creating a trust. Because the minor is the owner of the account, it counts as his asset on the FAFSA, not the asset of the custodian, who is often the parent."[28]

A UGMA and UTMA are examples of a **Giftrust,** a special form of trust that holds the parents' *gift* in an account as a trust for the beneficiary. It has a Taxpayer Identification Number (TIN) instead of a Social Security Number. Even if the student does not have access, the student is the *owner* and reports it as an asset.

In a **Custodial Account**, a custodian manages the account for a beneficiary who is a minor. These are also considered *assets of the student*, to be reported on the FAFSA, even if the student has no control or access until age 18 or 21.

Unfortunately, students are assessed on assets that they may not have access to. A possible solution is to move money from these accounts into a 529 Plan, an educational account. Ask questions before maturity because once students gain control, consent must be given for the organization to discuss concerns with parents.

Example: Anna has a $10,000 trust which she will not have access to until age 21. For the first base year, this trust is assessed at 20 percent, so Anna's aid is reduced by $2,000. Anna must come up with $2,000 for school, yet she cannot take it from her trust. The second through fourth year, this process repeats. Essentially Anna loses $8,000 ($2,000 per year × 4 years) in potential aid, because she owns but cannot touch her trust.

If the trust can be liquidated, and in turn, the proceeds placed into a 529 Plan owned by the student, you create a parent asset. In turn, for the year of liquidation (hopefully not a base year), any gains are reported on the student tax return, and thus included in the student's AGI.

---

28. Application and Verification Guide 2013-2014, *Filling out the FAFSA,* "Trusts," p. 19, http://ifap.ed.gov/fsahandbook/attachments/1314AVG.pdf

Tax Strategies and Benefits

Taxes and Investments

Consider the following when choosing where to invest and save:

1. Whose asset will it be in the EFC calculations?

2. Will distributions be declared as income and to whom?

3. What is the growth potential and risk of the investment?

4. Do you have control of the type of investments held within the account (bonds, stocks, mutual funds, etc.)?

5. Does this investment balance out your financial portfolio?

6. Does the account have tax benefits that you can qualify for?

IRS Publication 970, *Tax Benefits for Education* defines who is an eligible student, what is an eligible educational institution, income limitations, and which expenses (tuition, books, room and board, supplies, etc.) are allowed when claiming each education tax benefit.

Try for 5 Years of Education Tax Benefits

Educational tax benefits are based on the calendar year. Typically this means four years of benefits. Usually the fall and upcoming spring semesters are paid by December 31. Instead, in the final year, see if your school will allow you to pay the spring semester of senior year during the first week of January, so the payment falls in the next calendar year. This creates five years:

1. Freshman fall + spring semesters paid by December 31

2. Sophomore fall + spring semesters paid by December 31

3. Junior fall + spring semesters paid by December 31

4. Senior fall semester paid by December 31

5. Senior spring semester paid the first week in January

A five year college payment calendar allows for five years of education benefits on a tax return. (*Note:* The American Opportunity Credit, discussed later, can only be claimed for four years, so another benefit would be chosen for year five.)

Education Tax Benefits

We previously discussed investments where the growth can be declared tax-free when used for eligible education expenses.

A different type of educational tax benefit can be claimed on your tax return for expenses paid with funds that did not qualify for any other sort of education tax exclusion or benefit.

These education benefits are:

1. Student Loan Interest Deduction

2. Tuition and Fees Deduction

3. American Opportunity Credit

4. Lifetime Learning Credit

Student Loan Interest can be claimed with the Tuition and Fees Deduction, the American Opportunity Credit, or the Lifetime Learning Credit for the same student; but you can claim *only one* of the latter three for the *same student* in the same year.

The front of Form 1040 contains both the Student Loan Interest Deduction (line 33) and a Tuition and Fees Deduction (line 34). You don't have to itemize to claim these, but the Tuition and Fees Deduction requires completion of Form 8917, Tuition and Fees Deduction. Both of these reduce your income subject to tax (AGI).

The reverse of the Form 1040 contains educational credits. They are applied *after taxes*, reducing your taxes dollar-for-dollar. The nonrefundable portion also reduces your EFC. The American Opportunity Credit (line 49, nonrefundable portion, and line 66, refundable portion) and the Lifetime Learning Credit (line 49; nonrefundable) are claimed on Form 8863, Education Credits. In general, it is preferable to claim an educational credit.

Your own personal goals play a role when choosing between these benefits. If you want to reduce your AGI (perhaps to qualify for the Automatic Zero EFC or Simplified Needs Test), try to take both deductions on the front of your return. If this does not make you eligible for a special EFC category, then you would aim to take the Student Loan Interest Deduction on the front of the Form 1040 and a credit on the reverse of the form. Credits lower your taxes by the maximum amount and are subtracted for your EFC.

When you are ineligible to claim a credit (due to income thresholds, half-time student status, etc.) you should try to take the two deduction options on the front.

Form 1040 (front)

Form **1040**	Department of the Treasury—Internal Revenue Service (99) **U.S. Individual Income Tax Return**	**2013**	OMB No. 1545-0074	IRS Use Only—Do not write or staple in this space.

For the year Jan. 1–Dec. 31, 2013, or other tax year beginning	, 2013, ending	, 20	See separate instructions.

Your first name and initial	Last name		Your social security number

If a joint return, spouse's first name and initial	Last name		Spouse's social security number

Home address (number and street). If you have a P.O. box, see instructions.	Apt. no.	▲ Make sure the SSN(s) above and on line 6c are correct.

City, town or post office, state, and ZIP code. If you have a foreign address, also complete spaces below (see instructions).

Presidential Election Campaign
Check here if you, or your spouse if filing jointly, want $3 to go to this fund. Checking a box below will not change your tax or refund. ☐ You ☐ Spouse

Foreign country name	Foreign province/state/county	Foreign postal code

Filing Status
Check only one box.

1 ☐ Single
2 ☐ Married filing jointly (even if only one had income)
3 ☐ Married filing separately. Enter spouse's SSN above and full name here. ▶
4 ☐ Head of household (with qualifying person). (See instructions.) If the qualifying person is a child but not your dependent, enter this child's name here. ▶
5 ☐ Qualifying widow(er) with dependent child

Exemptions

6a ☐ **Yourself.** If someone can claim you as a dependent, **do not** check box 6a
b ☐ **Spouse**
c **Dependents:**

(1) First name Last name	(2) Dependent's social security number	(3) Dependent's relationship to you	(4) ✓ If child under age 17 qualifying for child tax credit (see instructions)
			☐
			☐
			☐

If more than four dependents, see instructions and check here ▶ ☐

Boxes checked on 6a and 6b ___
No. of children on 6c who:
• lived with you ___
• did not live with you due to divorce or separation (see instructions) ___
Dependents on 6c not entered above ___
Add numbers on lines above ▶ ___

d Total number of exemptions claimed

Income

Attach Form(s) W-2 here. Also attach Forms W-2G and 1099-R if tax was withheld.

If you did not get a W-2, see instructions.

7	Wages, salaries, tips, etc. Attach Form(s) W-2	7	
8a	**Taxable interest.** Attach Schedule B if required	8a	
b	Tax-exempt interest. **Do not** include on line 8a	8b	
9a	Ordinary dividends. Attach Schedule B if required	9a	
b	Qualified dividends	9b	
10	Taxable refunds, credits, or offsets of state and local income taxes	10	
11	Alimony received	11	
12	Business income or (loss). Attach Schedule C or C-EZ	12	
13	Capital gain or (loss). Attach Schedule D if required. If not required, check here ▶ ☐	13	
14	Other gains or (losses). Attach Form 4797	14	
15a	IRA distributions 15a	b Taxable amount	15b	
16a	Pensions and annuities 16a	b Taxable amount	16b	
17	Rental real estate, royalties, partnerships, S corporations, trusts, etc. Attach Schedule E	17	
18	Farm income or (loss). Attach Schedule F	18	
19	Unemployment compensation	19	
20a	Social security benefits 20a	b Taxable amount	20b	
21	Other income. List type and amount	21	
22	Combine the amounts in the far right column for lines 7 through 21. This is your **total income** ▶	22	

Adjusted Gross Income

23	Educator expenses	23	
24	Certain business expenses of reservists, performing artists, and fee-basis government officials. Attach Form 2106 or 2106-EZ	24	
25	Health savings account deduction. Attach Form 8889	25	
26	Moving expenses. Attach Form 3903	26	
27	Deductible part of self-employment tax. Attach Schedule SE	27	
28	Self-employed SEP, SIMPLE, and qualified plans	28	
29	Self-employed health insurance deduction	29	
30	Penalty on early withdrawal of savings	30	
31a	Alimony paid b Recipient's SSN ▶	31a	
32	IRA deduction	32	
33	Student loan interest deduction	33	
34	Tuition and fees. Attach Form 8917	34	
35	Domestic production activities deduction. Attach Form 8903	35	
36	Add lines 23 through 35	36	
37	Subtract line 36 from line 22. This is your **adjusted gross income** ▶	37	

For Disclosure, Privacy Act, and Paperwork Reduction Act Notice, see separate instructions.   Cat. No. 11320B   Form **1040** (2013)

Education Deductions

Form 1040 (reverse)

Form 1040 (2013)				Page **2**

Tax and	38	Amount from line 37 (adjusted gross income)	38	
Credits	39a	Check if: ☐ You were born before January 2, 1949, ☐ Blind. ☐ Spouse was born before January 2, 1949, ☐ Blind. Total boxes checked ► 39a		
	b	If your spouse itemizes on a separate return or you were a dual-status alien, check here ► 39b ☐		
Standard Deduction for—	40	**Itemized deductions** (from Schedule A) **or your standard deduction** (see left margin)	40	
• People who check any box on line 39a or 39b or who can be claimed as a dependent, see instructions.	41	Subtract line 40 from line 38	41	
	42	**Exemptions.** If line 38 is $150,000 or less, multiply $3,900 by the number on line 6d. Otherwise, see instructions	42	
	43	**Taxable income.** Subtract line 42 from line 41. If line 42 is more than line 41, enter -0-	43	
	44	**Tax** (see instructions). Check if any from: a ☐ Form(s) 8814 b ☐ Form 4972 c ☐ ___	44	
	45	**Alternative minimum tax** (see instructions). Attach Form 6251	45	
• All others:	46	Add lines 44 and 45 ►	46	
Single or Married filing separately, $6,100	47	Foreign tax credit. Attach Form 1116 if required	47	
	48	Credit for child and dependent care expenses. Attach Form 2441	48	
	49	Education credits from Form 8863, line 19	49	◄
Married filing jointly or Qualifying widow(er), $12,200	50	Retirement savings contributions credit. Attach Form 8880	50	
	51	Child tax credit. Attach Schedule 8812, if required	51	
	52	Residential energy credits. Attach Form 5695	52	
Head of household, $8,950	53	Other credits from Form: a ☐ 3800 b ☐ 8801 c ☐ ___	53	
	54	Add lines 47 through 53. These are your **total credits**	54	
	55	Subtract line 54 from line 46. If line 54 is more than line 46, enter -0- ►	55	
Other Taxes	56	Self-employment tax. Attach Schedule SE	56	
	57	Unreported social security and Medicare tax from Form: a ☐ 4137 b ☐ 8919	57	
	58	Additional tax on IRAs, other qualified retirement plans, etc. Attach Form 5329 if required	58	
	59a	Household employment taxes from Schedule H	59a	
	b	First-time homebuyer credit repayment. Attach Form 5405 if required	59b	
	60	Taxes from: a ☐ Form 8959 b ☐ Form 8960 c ☐ Instructions; enter code(s) _____	60	
	61	Add lines 55 through 60. This is your **total tax** ►	61	
Payments	62	Federal income tax withheld from Forms W-2 and 1099	62	
	63	2013 estimated tax payments and amount applied from 2012 return	63	
If you have a qualifying child, attach Schedule EIC.	64a	**Earned income credit (EIC)**	64a	
	b	Nontaxable combat pay election 64b		
	65	Additional child tax credit. Attach Schedule 8812	65	
	66	American opportunity credit from Form 8863, line 8	66	◄
	67	Reserved	67	
	68	Amount paid with request for extension to file	68	
	69	Excess social security and tier 1 RRTA tax withheld	69	
	70	Credit for federal tax on fuels. Attach Form 4136	70	
	71	Credits from Form: a ☐ 2439 b ☐ Reserved c ☐ 8885 d ☐	71	
	72	Add lines 62, 63, 64a, and 65 through 71. These are your **total payments** ►	72	
Refund	73	If line 72 is more than line 61, subtract line 61 from line 72. This is the amount you **overpaid**	73	
	74a	Amount of line 73 you want **refunded to you.** If Form 8888 is attached, check here ► ☐	74a	
Direct deposit? See instructions.	b	Routing number		
	d	Account number ► c Type: ☐ Checking ☐ Savings		
	75	Amount of line 73 you want **applied to your 2014 estimated tax** ► 75		
Amount You Owe	76	**Amount you owe.** Subtract line 72 from line 61. For details on how to pay, see instructions ►	76	
	77	Estimated tax penalty (see instructions) 77		

Third Party Designee	Do you want to allow another person to discuss this return with the IRS (see instructions)? ☐ Yes. Complete below. ☐ No Designee's name ► Phone no. ► Personal identification number (PIN) ►
Sign Here Joint return? See instructions. Keep a copy for your records.	Under penalties of perjury, I declare that I have examined this return and accompanying schedules and statements, and to the best of my knowledge and belief, they are true, correct, and complete. Declaration of preparer (other than taxpayer) is based on all information of which preparer has any knowledge. Your signature / Date / Your occupation / Daytime phone number Spouse's signature. If a joint return, **both** must sign. / Date / Spouse's occupation / If the IRS sent you an Identity Protection PIN, enter it here (see inst.)
Paid Preparer Use Only	Print/Type preparer's name / Preparer's signature / Date / Check ☐ if self-employed / PTIN Firm's name ► Firm's EIN ► Firm's address ► Phone no.

Form **1040** (2013)

Education Credits

Student Loan Interest Deduction

Student Loan Interest Deduction is a deduction of up to $2,500 *per tax return* for interest paid on qualified loans.

Some student loans require interest payments immediately, rather than waiting until after graduation. The Student Loan Interest Deduction can always be claimed in addition to the other education benefits: the Tuition and Fees Deduction, American Opportunity Credit or Lifetime Learning Credit for the same student; but you can claim only one of the latter three for the same student in the same year. (Per IRS Publications 17 and 970)

You are generally permitted to deduct the interest amount or $2,500, whichever is less. Your 2013 **Modified Adjusted Gross Income (MAGI)** (defined p. 99) must be under $75,000 ($155,000 for joint returns). Who can claim the deduction is discussed later (*See* p. 116).

Student Loan Interest Table

Feature	Description
Maximum benefit	You can reduce your income subject to tax by up to $2,500.
Loan qualifications	Your student loan: • must have been taken out solely to pay qualified education expenses, and • cannot be from a related person or made under a qualified employer plan.
Student qualifications	The student must be: • you, your spouse, or your dependent, and • enrolled at least half-time in a program leading to a degree, certificate, or other recognized educational credential at an eligible educational institution.
Time limit on deduction	You can deduct interest paid during the remaining period of your student loan.
Phaseout	The amount of your deduction depends on your income level.

Tuition and Fees Deduction

The Tuition and Fees Deduction allows you to deduct qualified educational expenses (personal, living, or family expenses, such as room and board are not included) for a student (regardless of year attending). You can claim up to $4,000 from income *per tax return* and it may be a sum of expenses from two separate students.

> *Example:* Two single students each claim $4,000 in expenses on their individual tax returns (using $8,000 of expenses), but once married, they can only claim $4,000 in expenses on their joint tax return. The limit is *per return*, not per person. If both students had $2,000 in expenses when married, they could each claim $2,000 for a $4,000 total.

Your Modified Adjusted Gross Income (MAGI) (defined p. 99) must be less than $80,000 ($160,000 if filing a joint return). [29]

Table 6-2. Effect of MAGI on Maximum Tuition and Fees Deduction		
IF your filing status is...	AND your MAGI is...	THEN your maximum tuition and fees deduction is...
single, head of household, or qualifying widow(er)	not more than $65,000	$4,000.
	more than $65,000 but not more than $80,000	$2,000.
	more than $80,000	$0.
married filing joint return	not more than $130,000	$4,000.
	more than $130,000 but not more than $160,000	$2,000.
	more than $160,000	$0.

The deduction is taken on the front of the tax form, reducing your AGI. Tax software programs and many preparers are only thinking about maximizing your return. They tend to think receiving the tax credits is always best.

However, it might be best to take the deduction if reducing your AGI would qualify you for the Automatic Zero EFC or the Simplified Needs Test (SNT). Compare the impact of taking the deduction for EFC purposes, with taking a credit for tax savings. Who can claim this deduction is discussed later (*See* p. 116).

---

29. IRS, Publication 970, Tax Benefits for Education, *Student Loan Interest Deduction*, p. 33 http://www.irs.gov/pub/irs-pdf/p970.pdf.

American Opportunity Credit

The American Opportunity Credit evolved from what used to be called the Hope Credit. It is a *partially refundable* credit for up to $4,000 of qualified expenses during the *first four years* of post-secondary education. (See qualified expenses in the table below.)

The credit is calculated on Form 8863, Education Credits. You receive 100% of the first $2,000 in expenses, plus 25% of the next $2,000, for a maximum credit of $2,500 *per student*. Up to $1,000 (40% × $2,500) is *refundable*, which means, even if you have no tax liability, you might receive up to $1,000 towards your tax refund. This refundable portion is not reported on the FAFSA. The non-refundable portion is an offset to income, lowering your EFC. (*See* p. 35 and worksheet line 6 p. 29)

Who can claim this credit is discussed later (*See* p. 114). Below is the summary Table from 2013 IRS Publication 17, p.225 (http://www.irs.gov/pub/irs-pdf/p17.pdf) with income and other rules noted.

	American Opportunity Credit
Maximum credit	Up to $2,500 credit per **eligible student**
Limit on modified adjusted gross income (MAGI)	$180,000 if married filing jointly; $90,000 if single, head of household, or qualifying widow(er)
Refundable or nonrefundable	40% of credit may be refundable
Number of years of postsecondary education	Available **ONLY** if the student had not completed the first 4 years of postsecondary education before 2013
Number of tax years credit available	Available **ONLY** for 4 tax years per eligible student (including any year(s) the Hope credit was claimed)
Type of program required	Student must be pursuing a program leading to a degree or other recognized education credential
Number of courses	Student must be enrolled at least half time for at least one academic period beginning during the tax year
Felony drug conviction	At the end of 2013, the student had not been convicted of a felony for possessing or distributing a controlled substance
Qualified expenses	Tuition, required enrollment fees, and course materials that the student needs for a course of study whether or not the materials are bought at the educational institution as a condition of enrollment or attendance
Payments for academic periods	Payments made in 2013 for academic periods beginning in 2013 or beginning in the first 3 months of 2014

Lifetime Learning Credit

The Lifetime Learning Credit is a *non-refundable* credit (meaning you must have a tax liability) for 20 percent of qualified expenses up to a limit of $2,000 *per tax return*. You can combine expenses from different students. To receive the full $2,000 credit, you would need $10,000 of qualified expenses.

An advantage of this credit is the education expenses can be undergraduate, graduate, and professional degree courses for a student regardless of year attending or if a half-time student.

Because this credit is 20 percent of total expenses, usually the American Opportunity Credit with the better 40 percent rate and which can be claimed *per student*, is a better deal (if you qualify).

Who can claim this credit is discussed later (*See* p. 114). Below is a summary Table from 2013 IRS Publication 17, p.225 (http://www.irs.gov/pub/irs-pdf/p17.pdf) with income and other rules noted.

	Lifetime Learning Credit
Maximum credit	Up to $2,000 credit per **return**
Limit on modified adjusted gross income (MAGI)	$127,000 if married filing jointly; $63,000 if single, head of household, or qualifying widow(er)
Refundable or nonrefundable	Credit limited to the amount of tax you must pay on your taxable income
Number of years of postsecondary education	Available for all years of postsecondary education and for courses to acquire or improve job skills
Number of tax years credit available	Available for an unlimited number of years
Type of program required	Student does not need to be pursuing a program leading to a degree or other recognized education credential
Number of courses	Available for one or more courses
Felony drug conviction	Felony drug convictions do not make the student ineligible
Qualified expenses	Tuition and fees required for enrollment or attendance (including amounts required to be paid to the institution for course-related books, supplies, and equipment)
Payments for academic periods	Payments made in 2013 for academic periods beginning in 2013 or beginning in the first 3 months of 2014

(Modified AGI is defined on p. 99.)

Who Claims the Education Credits & Deductions?

American Opportunity and Lifetime Learning Credits

The American Opportunity and Lifetime Learning Credits have some similarities in their eligibility rules for claiming tax benefits.

> "If an exemption is allowed as a deduction for any person who claims the student as a dependent, all qualified education expenses of the student are treated as having been paid by that person. Therefore, only that person can claim an education credit for the student. If a student is not claimed as a dependent on another person's tax return, only the student can claim a credit."[30]

This table combined from IRS Publication 970 (p.15 & 23), http://www.irs.gov/pub/irs-pdf/p970.pdf is also helpful:

IF you...	THEN only...	THEN only...
claim an exemption on your tax return for a dependent who is an eligible student	you can claim the American opportunity credit based on that dependent's expenses. The dependent cannot claim the credit.	you can claim the lifetime learning credit based on that dependent's expenses. The dependent cannot claim the credit.
do **not** claim an exemption on your tax return for a dependent who is an eligible student (even if entitled to the exemption)	the dependent can claim the American opportunity credit. You cannot claim the credit based on this dependent's expenses.	the dependent can claim the lifetime learning credit. You cannot claim the credit based on this dependent's expenses.

If parents choose not to claim a student (eligible dependent), the parents give up the dependency exemption along with all other dependency related benefits. By doing this, the student can claim the educational credit, but not the exemption (and usually not the refundable portion of the American Opportunity Credit), regardless of who actually paid for the expenses.

Students can never claim their own exemption when parents are eligible, but choose not to claim the exemption. When parents choose to give the educational credit to the student, the dependency exemption is lost. No one claims it.

Parents might pass the educational credit if they exceed the income threshold for eligibility, and they don't care about the impact of losing the student exemption on their own return.

You might run different scenarios to determine the best financial outcome for the family. Be sure to also look at your state return.

30. IRS, Publication 17, 2013, Your Federal Income Tax, *Education Credits*, "Who Can Claim an Education Credit," p. 224. http://www.irs.gov/pub/irs-pdf/p17.pdf

Third Party, Inheritance, Divorce, etc., and the Credits

The parent claiming the student dependency exemption has the right to claim the educational credit, *regardless of who actually paid the expenses*. If the expenses were paid by a noncustodial parent, grandparent, friend, or inheritance, the custodial parent can still claim the credit.

> "Qualified education expenses paid on behalf of the student by someone other than the student (*such as a relative*) are treated as paid by the student. Qualified education expenses paid (or treated as paid) by a student who is claimed as *a dependent on your tax return are treated as paid by you.*"[31]

Therefore, you are treated as having paid expenses that were paid from your dependent student's earnings, gifts, inheritances, savings, etc.

This only applies to the education *credits*. For the deductions, *it does matter* who paid the bill.

A custodial parent is able to release the dependency exemption, to allow the noncustodial parent to claim an educational credit. For divorces finalized after 2009, the release *must be* accomplished by completing and signing IRS Form 8332, Release/Revocation of Release of Claim to Exemption for Child by Custodial Parent. (See instructions at http://www.irs.gov/pub/irs-pdf/f8332.pdf)

Often, the parents agree to share the refund obtained by the noncustodial parent. Sharing can also be required by a court order. When the Form 8332 is signed, the custodial parent keeps the:

- Filing status
- Credit for Child and Dependent Care Expenses (for children under age 13)
- Earned Income Credit (EIC)

The noncustodial parent receives the right (assuming eligibility requirements are met) to claim the:

- Dependent exemption
- Child Tax Credit and Additional Child Tax Credit (for children under age 17)
- Educational benefits

---

31. IRS, Publication 17, 2013, *Your Federal Income Tax, Qualified Education Expenses*, p. 225. http://www.irs.gov/pub/irs-pdf/p17.pdf

Student Loan Interest Deduction

To claim the Student Loan Interest Deduction, the taxpayer must:

1. Not file Married Filing Separately,

2. Not only have paid the interest, but

3. Was legally obligated to pay the interest, and

4. *Not have been claimed* as an exemption on another return.

The only way for a student to claim the deduction is if the parents give up the dependency exemption. If a student meets all the conditions except a third party (parent, grandparent, or organization) paid the interest, then the student is considered to have paid the interest and takes the deduction.[32]

Credit card interest can be claimed as student loan interest if the credit card is solely used for college expenses. The best way to do this is to open a separate account used only for school. If you have mixed transactions on a card, the interest cannot be claimed as you would be unable to allocate how much interest is school related and how much belongs to other purchases.

Tuition and Fees Deduction

To claim the Tuition and Fees Deduction, generally:

1. You paid qualified education expenses of higher education in 2013 for academic periods beginning in 2013 and those beginning in the first three months of 2014.

2. You paid the education expenses for an eligible student.

3. The eligible student is yourself, your spouse, or your dependent *for whom you claim an exemption* .

However, there are some exceptions.
  "You cannot take the deduction if any of the following apply.

1. Your filing status is married filing separately.

2. Another person can claim an exemption for you as a dependent on his or her tax return. (You cannot take the deduction even if the other person does not actually claim that exemption.)

---

32. IRS, Publication 170, 2013, Your Federal Income Tax, *Student Loan Interest Deduction*, p. 137 http://www.irs.gov/pub/irs-pdf/p17.pdf

3. Your modified adjusted gross income (MAGI) is more than $80,000 ($160,000 if filing a joint return).

4. You (or your spouse) were a nonresident alien for any part of 2013 and the nonresident alien did not elect to be treated as a resident alien for tax purposes. More information on nonresident aliens can be found in Publication 519, U.S. Tax Guide for Aliens.

5. You or anyone else claims an American Opportunity or Lifetime Learning credit in 2013 with respect to expenses of the student for whom the qualified education expenses were paid. However, a state tax credit will not disqualify you from claiming a tuition and fees deduction."[33]

When parents claim the student exemption and *the parents pay* the expenses, the parents can claim the deduction. If the student paid the expenses, no one can take the deduction. The only time a student can claim the deduction is if the student is *not eligible* to be claimed on the parents' tax return, and in such a case, it does not matter who (the student or parents) paid the bill

To Claim the Tuition and Fees Deduction for a Dependent

IF your dependent is an eligible student and you...	AND...	THEN...
claim an exemption for your dependent	you paid all qualified education expenses for your dependent	only you can deduct the qualified education expenses that you paid. Your dependent cannot take a deduction.
claim an exemption for your dependent	your dependent paid all qualified education expenses	no one is allowed to take a deduction.
do not claim an exemption for your dependent	you paid all qualified education expenses	no one is allowed to take a deduction.
do not claim an exemption for your dependent	your dependent paid all qualified education expenses	no one is allowed to take a deduction.

33. Ibid., *Tuition and Fees*, "Can You Claim the Deduction," p. 138,

No Double Dipping

Exploring different tax benefits may provide more options to obtain cash for college. If eligible, you might use these ideas to decrease your AGI and impact the EFC or increase your refund.

> *Example:* If you have $4,000 in college expenses and you are eligible to use these expenses to claim the American Opportunity Credit, and you have a tax liability of at least $2,500, you will receive $2,500 back. This credit is a dollar-for-dollar return on your tax liability. You reduced your college expenses to $1,500 ($4,000 expenses − $2,500 credit). Even if your tax liability was zero, you would still qualify for a partial refund of $1,000 back.

You can only claim (receive) one tax benefit per education expense.

> "An American opportunity or lifetime learning credit (education credit) can be claimed in the same year the beneficiary takes a tax-free distribution from a QTP, as long as the same expenses are not used for both benefits.."[34]

The easiest way to track this is to match education receipts to one of three tax benefits (exclusions, student loan interest, or either a credit or deduction). After each match, you will need new, different receipts (expenses) to claim another education benefit.

> *Example:* College expenses are $9,000. You cashed $9,000 of EE Bonds for school. You qualify for the American Opportunity Credit, but to claim the bond interest as tax-free you must declare the full $9,000 of proceeds against expenses. This leaves no expenses left to allocate for the credit. If possible, you should have cashed only $5,000 in bonds and paid $4,000 of expenses from savings or your income, so you could receive the $2,500 credit.

When you pay for educational expenses from funds that have no other tax benefit, these funds and expenses are eligible to be used toward either the deduction or a credit. When you pay for expenses with funds from education tax exclusion accounts, those accounts already have a tax benefit, so they can't be used to receive education deductions or credits.

---

34. IRS, Publication 970, Tax Benefits for Education, *American Opportunity Credit,* " p. 11, http://www.irs.gov/pub/irs-pdf/p970.pdf

You also have to actually *pay (or be treated as having paid)* for the educational expenses. If a student's tuition was $3,000 but a scholarship was received for $2,000, then there is only $1,000 of educational expenses to be used to claim either a tax exclusion or an education benefit (deduction or credit). Only $1,000 was paid.

Education expenses are claimed for benefits during the year in which tuition is paid. This isn't necessarily the year a loan repayment is made. There is also a 3 month rule for expenses paid in one year for the first three months of the following year.

> *Example:* Qualified expenses paid in 2013 for an academic period that begins in the first 3 months of 2014 can only be used in figuring your 2013 education tax benefits.

Keep track of all expenses (tuition, room and board, supplies, books, computers, etc.) and who paid for them (parents, non-custodial parent, student, grant, scholarship, gift, loans, or other means). Also keep a record if funds went directly to the school, store, or student (who in turn made the purchase).

It's worthwhile to run different scenarios using tax software. If you are not trying to reduce your AGI to qualify to exclude assets, then you should aim to take an education credit. You might also run scenarios for the upcoming the year to decide when to pay for spring tuition. To plan your payments ahead of time, you would want to decide:

1. What is the most favorable education benefit (deduction or a credit) that you intend to qualify for by allocating money that had no tax exclusion benefits?

2. Which expenses will be used against this benefit? (Recall some tax benefits only permit tuition expenses, not room and board.)

3. Once you have allocated expenses to either a credit or a deduction, do you have remaining expenses that you can plan to pay from an asset that has a tax-exclusion benefit?

4. If you plan to withdraw assets or take distributions how will this impact next years EFC and next years taxes?

Every time you consider a financial movement, you should ask how it will affect your taxes, how it will affect your family EFC, and how will it impact your future retirement?

Other Credits

Retirement Savings Contribution Credit

The Retirement Savings Contribution Credit, also called the Saver's Credit, is restricted based on your age, filing status, tax liability, and your Adjusted Gross Income, AGI.

For tax year 2013, your AGI may not be more than:

- $29,500 if you file Single, Married Filing Separately, or Qualifying Widow(er)
- $44,250 if you file Head of Household, or
- $59,000 if you file Married Filing Jointly[35]

This is a *nonrefundable* credit, meaning you must have taxable income to receive it. You must also be at least age 18, not a full-time student, and not claimed as a dependent on another tax return.

While dependent students cannot claim the credit, it might be available to Independent Students and graduate students who are not going to school full time. Dependent students should be aware of the credit so they can take advantage of it upon graduation.

Parents can also qualify. Parents usually have to watch their AGI when aiming to meet the eligibility requirements.

The credit is worth up to $1,000 ($2,000 for MFJ) and you qualify by meeting the criteria above and making an eligible contribution to a qualified retirement plan. The previously discussed employer matching plans and IRAs count as qualified retirement plans.

The credit you receive ranges from 10 to 50 percent of your total contributions made during the tax year, up to a maximum credit of $1,000. The percentage awarded is based on your income and filing status. Form 8880, *Credit for Qualified Retirement Savings Contributions* is used to compute your rate and claim the credit.

The credit is essentially money back for contributing to these plans. Simply put, if you invested $5,000 in an IRA and qualify for a $1,000 credit, it's as if your IRA only cost you $4,000. It's like the government is funding your retirement. At tax filing time, check if funding (or partially funding) an IRA makes you eligible for this credit. Occasionally, contributing $1,000 gives you a $500 credit.

---

35. IRS, Retirement Topics, *Retirement Savings Contributions Credit,* http://www.irs.gov/retirement/participant/article/0,,id=211619,00.html

Earned Income Credit (EIC)

The Earned Income Credit is a *refundable* credit. This means you can receive it even if you have no tax liability.

You must be between 25 and 65 years of age, have *earned income* (alimony does not count), have a valid Social Security Number, not be a qualifying dependent, meet certain income requirements, and not have investment income above a certain amount ($3,300 in 2013).

You can claim the Earned Income Credit if you file single, Head of Household or Married Filing Jointly (MFJ). The 2013 earned income and AGI limits for EIC are:

- $46,227 ($51,567 for MFJ) with three or more qualifying children,
- $43,038 ($48,378 for MFJ) with two qualifying children,
- $37,870 ($43,210 for MFJ) with one qualifying child, or
- $14,340 ($19,680 for MFJ) with no qualifying child.

The maximum earned income credit for 2013 is:

- $6,044 with three or more qualifying children;
- $5,372 with two qualifying children;
- $3,250 with one qualifying child; and
- $487 with no qualifying children.[36]

Many undergraduate students do not qualify due to their age (under age 25) and the requirement to *not* be a dependent, but some students will be age 25 in their senior year. Perhaps they started school late, repeated a year, or took a year off to volunteer abroad. If the student meets the criteria, this is more money (especially if the student has a child) that can be used toward college expenses or loans.

Parents can focus on the eligibility criteria as well, checking how they could influence their income or investments to not only qualify for EIC, but maximize the amount received. (*See* Life insurance impacting EIC, Example p. 88)

---

36. IRS, Publication 596, *Earned Income Credit*, http://www.irs.gov/pub/irs-pdf/p596.pdf

Student's Income and Loss of Dependency

Student income can affect dependency on your tax return. This book assumes the student is *unmarried* and qualifies as an eligible student (*See* p.126). Five requirements must be met for a student to be a qualifying child claimed for the IRS dependency exemption:

1. *Relationship:* A dependent student is the parents' biological child, stepchild, adopted child, or eligible foster child (placed by a legal agency).

2. *Age:* The student is under age 19, or a full time student between age 19-24, or a permanently disabled child.

3. *Residency:* The students lives with the parents for more than half the year with exceptions for temporary absences, such as school and divorced parents.

4. *Support:* The student "cannot have provided more than half his or her support."[37]

5. *Dependency:* The parent (taxpayer) cannot be claimed as a dependent.

The following example will be used to discuss support:

> *Example:* Nineteen year-old Nicole, a student, earned $10,000 for her acting career this year. She lives with her parents who earned $60,000.

Dependency will rely on whether or not Nicole paid over half her support. Support include all funds spent on a child in any fashion, including food, clothing, shelter, education, medical care, recreation, and transportation. If the total cost of supporting Nicole this year was $15,000, and Nicole's $10,000 was spent on her, then Nicole provided over half her own support. Her parents cannot claim her for the dependency exemption or education benefits.

If Nicole saved her earnings, she qualifies as a dependent.

> "A person's own funds are not support unless they are actually spent for support."[38]

---

37. IRS Publication 501, Exemptions, Standard Deduction and Filing Information, *Support Test to be a Qualifying Child*, p. 13, http://www.irs.gov/pub/irs-pdf/p501.pdf

38. Ibid, *Support Test to be a Qualifying Relative*, "Persons own funds not used for support," p.17.

Child stars or entrepreneurs are not the only scenario.

> *Example:* A single parent earns $20,000. Her student (son) earns $6,000 and spends all his earnings on himself. To keep the dependency exemption, his total support for the year must be over $12,000, because his $6,000 spent cannot be more than half his support. This leaves the parent with only $8,000 for herself, unless she is also living on savings. This student may not be a dependent.

Parents who hire their children to work in the family business or as household employees can't include these wages as support:

> "You cannot include in *your* contribution to your child's support any support that is paid for by the child with the child's own wages, even if you paid the wages."[39]

If you paid your son to mow the lawn and he spends those dollars on himself, that money is considered support provided *by your child.*

Parents, who want to claim the dependency and educational benefits for their working students, might monitor their child's earnings and encourage saving rather than spending to be sure their child is not paying over half of his or her own support.

Some parents may *want* their child to claim the education benefit. Recall that parents can forgo claiming an exemption to let the student claim an education credit, but for the student to claim the Tuition and Fees Deduction, the student must qualify to claim his or her own exemption. If parents allow students to provide over half of their own support, these students can claim the deduction. A student could work more hours or sell bonds and trusts, and this money belonging to the child would be spent on the child.

Before you help your child provide over 50 percent of his or her own support, check you medical insurance policy. Often medical insurance for children requires parents to provide over 50 percent support. Don't sacrifice medical insurance for a tax deduction.

Also, just because your student isn't considered a dependent child for taxes, does not make your student Independent for EFC purposes. Student aid and Federal income tax use different rules.

---

39. Ibid, "Child's wages used for own support," p. 17.

Student Loans, Scholarships, and Dependency

Five rules must be met for a student to be considered a qualifying child to be claimed for a dependency exemption (*See* p. 122). This exemption can be lost when students begin taking loans.

Student loans play a role because they interfere with the rule that requires a student to *not* provide more than half of his or her own support. If a loan is attributable to the student, it counts as support the student provides for his or herself.

To determine who provided what support, funds spent on a child in any fashion, including food, clothing, shelter, education, medical care, recreation, and transportation, must be attributed to coming from the student, parents, or other source. A student loan would be considered an "other" source.

Consider the following when accounting for support:

• *Savings and investments:* If a student removes money from savings, this is support provided by the student.

• *Earned income:* If the employed student is spending the earned income on his or herself, the income counts as support provided by the student. It does not matter if the money is spent on tuition, food, parties, or a car.

• *Gifts to the child spent on the child:* If Grandma gives the student $1,000 which is spent by the student, these funds count as support provided by the student.

• *Student Loans:* If the student takes a student loan out in his or her name, this counts as support provided by the student.[40]

• *Scholarships:* **do not count** at all as support

> "A scholarship received by a child who is a full-time student is not taken into account in determining whether the child provided more than half of his or her own support."[41]

---

40. IRS Publication 501, Exemptions, Standard Deduction and Filing Information, *Qualifying Relative*, "Support Test (To be a qualifying relative) Example 2" p. 20. http://www.irs.gov/pub/irs-pdf/p501.pdf

41. Ibid, *Qualifying Child*, "Support Test (to be a Qualifying Child) Scholarships" p. 15.

Example: Student Loans Affecting Support

Scott, a freshman in college, had these yearly costs:
$24,000 for tuition
$10,000 for rent
$ 4,000 for food and entertainment
$ 3,000 for miscellaneous expenses

$41,000 total expenses for Scott, the student
−$ 5,000 paid by scholarship

$36,000 total expenses for Scott, the student

    $16,000 was paid by a student loan (parent co-signed)
    $ 6,000 was paid by the student from his job
    $ 3,000 was paid by federal loans

    $25,000 total Scott, the student paid toward his support.

    $11,000 was paid by his parents.

The total expenses for Scott were reduced to $36,000 due to his scholarship not counting in support calculations.

The final totals show Scott paid $25,000 of his support, and his parents paid only $11,000.

Since Scott is considered to have paid over 50 percent of his support, he is no longer a qualifying child. His parents cannot claim him for a dependent exemption and his parents lose any other related benefits (such as education benefits) as well.

If Scott was the only son of a single parent, this parent has also lost the preferable filing status of Head of Household because this filing status requires the parent to have a qualifying child.

The single parent, might argue that the loan was co-signed so it's unfair to allocate it as Scott's contribution toward his support. This parent is also legally responsible for the loan. Unfortunately, at the moment, the IRS has made no concessions for co-signed loans. At the moment the parent is only the back-up and the student is the responsible party for the loan. The assumption is that all will go well, the student will repay the loan, and thus, the loan is allocated as support provided by the student.

This general example demonstrates how student loans can affect the dependency exemption on parents' taxes. Knowing these rules ahead of time allows you to plan ahead and avoid surprises when filing your taxes.

Sometimes there may be support and exemption questions concerning relatives. If certain criteria are met, a qualifying relative can be claimed for the dependency exemption. Student loans can interfere here as well.

> *Example:* "Your niece takes out a student loan of $2,500 and uses it to pay her college tuition. She is personally responsible for the loan. You provide $2,000 toward her total support. You cannot claim an exemption for her because you provide less than half of her support."[42]

IRS Definition of a Qualifying Student

The IRS describes a qualifying student for the purpose of the dependency exemption as:

> "To qualify as a student, your child must be, during some part of each of any 5 calendar months of the year:
>
> 1. A *full-time* student at a school that has a regular teaching staff, course of study, and a regularly enrolled student body at the school, or
>
> 2. A student taking a full-time, on-farm training course given by a school described in (1), or by a state, county, or local government agency.
>
> The 5 calendar months do not have to be consecutive."[43]

---

42. IRS Publication 501, Exemptions, Standard Deductions and Filing Information, *Qualifying Relative*, "Support Test to be a Qualifying Relative," http://www.irs.gov/pub/irs-pdf/p501.pdf

43. Ibid, *Qualifying Child*, "Student Defined,"

State Aid & State Tax Savings

Some states offer fantastic need-based aid. Sometimes parents must apply as early as middle school, so it's important to research state aid in the lower grades before the high school years..

Inquire at your state financial aid office to see what programs your state offers. Here are some examples:

1. *Florida* offers the merit-based Florida Bright Futures Scholarship Program which pays up to 100 percent of the required hours for a student's program of study. It has three lottery-funded scholarships to reward Florida high school graduates for high academic achievement.[44]

2. *Indiana* has the need-based Twenty-first Century Scholars Program which pays up to four years of undergraduate college tuition at eligible Indiana schools. You must apply in either the seventh, or eighth grade.[45]

Before you decide to move your family to a state to qualify for need-based aid, remember rules may change by the time you arrive. Also recall, residing in any state for four years will meet any state's criteria for state aid, but if you have lived in a state for less than that, you may not meet residency requirements.

Sometimes contributing to your state's 529 Plan will provide you with state tax savings. A percent of your contributions might be tax deductible up to your tax liability or a designated amount, usually whichever is less. Sometimes during the college years, parents can contribute to a 529 Plan in the same year they make a withdrawal and still save on state taxes. Sometimes even a rollover will count for 529 Plan state tax credits. Every state has unique rules.

You do not have to invest in your local 529 Plan. Compare 529 Plans for across different states to search for the best plans. (Keep in mind that out-of-state plans usually do not qualify for state tax savings.)

---

44. Florida Student Financial Aid, http://www.floridastudentfinancialaid. org/ssfad/home/ProgramsOffered.htm

45. Indiana.gov, Twenty-First Century Scholars, http://www. in.gov/21stcenturyscholars/

Where to Save First

When saving for college, consider how much you can afford to put away each month and how long it will be there with the potential to grow. Begin by considering excluded asset accounts and educational accounts, all the while considering their related tax benefits. The goal is to save in excluded assets that grow either tax-free or tax-deferred, while having either full access to or at least few restrictions on the use of your money.

Parents' retirement accounts should come first because:

1. You can borrow for college, but you can't borrow for retirement (except in the case of whole life insurance).

2. Parents often have employer matching plans, in which case saving for the parents' retirement results in a dollar-for-dollar growth, a 100 percent return on investment.

3. Financially secure parents will not be a burden on the student in later years.

4. Retirement accounts meet the goal of having an excluded asset, with some access to the funds, and tax benefits.

5. Funding the parents' retirement account *is saving* for the student's education. Every dollar set aside for the parents' retirement helps the student gain more aid, because it's one less dollar to be assessed by the EFC formula. Every shielded dollar brings the student more aid.

Invest in employer matching plans up to the match amount. Then, consider a Roth IRA. It grows tax-free with great flexibility, and can continue to grow if properly passed to heirs. During the base years, consider switching to a Traditional IRA if it reduces your AGI enough to qualify for the Automatic Zero EFC or SNT.

Life insurance might come next because it is again an excluded asset, with full access to funds and grows with tax benefits.

Educational accounts are especially good if contributions qualify for state tax benefits or if family income excludes you from other tax benefits. The same can be said for EE/I Bonds, but they have an additional benefit of no exclusive use.

Family goals, personal preferences, and comfort with risk will always play a factor. The best place to save depends on *you*.

What to Spend First

Choosing what to spend first is easy. Spend the student's assets first. What to spend next is more complicated. Suppose you have:

- Retirement Funds (employer matching and IRAs)
- Relatives who wish to help with college expenses
- Stocks or Mutual Funds with gains
- Life Insurance
- EE Bonds
- Education Accounts

Your last choice should be retirement fund withdrawals. As explained, these decrease funds available at retirement time and withdrawals increase income which increases your EFC.

Relatives should be instructed to postpone helping until after the FAFSA is signed for senior year or until after graduation. Third party support can increase the student EFC and reduce aid.

First spend funds from an account that qualifies for an educational tax deduction or credit on your tax return (assuming you are eligible). In the scenario above, the accounts that qualify are:

a. The spent student asset: if it was money spent from savings, income, or a trust (*not* an educational account)

b. Your stocks: However, the gains from sale will be counted as income for next year's EFC calculation

c. Your life insurance: where you borrow and pay interest but the EFC will be unaffected

Try to spend just enough from these accounts to maximize the "free money" you can receive taking a tax deduction or credit. For the American Opportunity Credit, spend only $4,000 to receive the $2,500 credit, or if you can't qualify for that, you might spend $10,000 to receive the maximum Lifetime Learning Credit of $2,000. (*Note:* If for some reason you took a loan large enough to receive a tax benefit, then consider holding these assets and move straight to spending educational accounts.)

Have a plan to exhaust your education account by graduation. Don't get stuck holding an account with restricted use. Keep your EE bonds as a later option, since they have no use restrictions.

What Will Your College Offer?

Research Your College

Finding the "Best Fit" is not just about college size, location, course offerings, and extra-curricular activities. You also want the best financial fit. Some high schools have a library containing college information to use for research, and sometimes college recruiters visit high schools to present informational slide shows.

When researching your college, ask about the cost and what the typical aid package includes: mostly *free* aid (which you do not have to repay) or loans. Also ask for copies of any additional aid forms required along with the FAFSA. These forms will immediately indicate if the college differs from the Federal Methodology (FM) when computing school aid awards. If your EFC is more than the Cost of Attendance (COA), ask about merit scholarships.

While two colleges might both claim to meet 100 percent of a student's need, perhaps the first school offers 80 percent in scholarship money and 20 percent in loans, and the second offers a 60/40 ratio. The second college is awarding more debt.

At http://www.collegeboard.com, if you enter a school in the college search box and click *Cost and Financial Aid,* you will see the school's financial statistics. Try to choose a college that offers a significant amount of *free* aid, rather than *self-help* aid which is a mix of loans and work-study. Colleges with huge endowments usually offer larger amounts of free aid. Because of this, a private school may be more affordable than a public one.

When you research a college's statistics, you can make a guess at the type of aid packet you might receive. If you choose a college that does not meet 100 percent of students' need, it's critical to realize you must pay your family EFC plus fulfill any *unmet need*.

The next example illustrates this. This family runs the calculations and finds they must fund an annual unmet need of $4,900, in addition to their $5,000 EFC. There is also $12,536 in self-help aid, part of which will be work-study but the other part will be debt (growing annually) that the student must repay after college. After realizing this, the student might look for scholarships to fulfill the unmet need or perhaps consider a different school (especially since these numbers do not include interest).

Example: In 2011, a Texas family with an EFC of $5,000 researches SUNY Binghampton. At http://www.collegeboard.com, entering the college name and clicking *Cost and Financial Aid*, the result for 2011 shows:

> Out-of-state tuition and fees: $15,291
> Room and board: $11,244
> Books and supplies: $ 800
> Estimated personal expenses: $ 750
> Transportation expense: $ 250
> Cost of Attendance (COA) $28,335
>
> *Average percent of need met:* **79 percent**
>
> *Financial Aid Distribution*
> Percent of total undergraduate aid awarded as:
> Scholarships / grants: **32 percent**
> Loans / jobs: **68 percent**

The Texas Family computes their financial need:

> COA: $28,335
> −EFC: $ 5,000
> Need: $23,335

The school (on average) will meet 79 percent of need:

Need:	$23,335	Need:	$23,335
Need Met:	*× 79%*	*Unmet:*	*× 21%*
Aid to Receive:	$18,435	**Unmet Need:**	**$ 4,900**

The school distributes the need amount as shown:

32 Percent in Scholarships: 32% × $18,435 = $ 5,899
68 Percent in Loans or Work: 68% × $18,435 = $12,536

To attend this school, the Texas family can expect to:

Pay their EFC of: $ 5,000
Somehow come up with annual unmet need of: $ 4,900
Take loans and work-study in the amount of: **$12,536**
Receive Scholarships in the amount of: $ 5,899
The total Cost Of Attendance (COA) is met for: $28,335

(*See also* p. 142)

By researching a college in the fall and computing estimates of future expenses, students can avoid applying to unaffordable schools. No parent wants to tell a child accepted at a *choice school,* "On second thought, we actually can't afford it. We didn't understand that they would offer so little free aid."

When a student is accepted at the unaffordable dream school, suddenly the parents become the reason the student can't attend. Parents feel guilty and begin to reflect on touching retirement funds, think about second jobs, and consider outrageous loans. You can avoid this situation entirely by researching schools, by discussing the concepts of free aid, self-help aid, and unmet need with your student, and by making smart decisions in the fall. This is one of the main goals of this book.

Students should apply to one or two safe schools. Safe schools are schools where the student not only expects to be admitted, but can also afford with little or no financial aid. They are usually a state school, because state aid plays a significant financial role.

Schools see every other school the student lists on the FAFSA, so they know who their competition is. If a student applies to only one school or applies as an *Early Decision* candidate, it appears the student will attend regardless of circumstances. There is no incentive for the school to offer substantial aid. On the other hand, if a school sees their competitor on the schools list, there is more incentive to prepare an attractive aid packet.

When researching a college, students should find ways to show interest and demonstrate that they bring more than good grades and study habits to the school. If contact is made with teachers or coaches, these people might in turn contact the admission or financial aid office to express the students' interest in the school or even better, to express their desire to have this student in their class or sport.

 Keep in mind the real job of the people assisting you. The college *Admissions Office* is paid to bring in the best students so the school can make claims concerning the incoming class. The *Financial Aid Office* is paid to protect school funds; not to provide students with the maximum amount of free aid possible. The high school *Guidance Counselor* is rated highly when graduates attend prestigious colleges. While they will all assist you, *not one* of them is paid to ensure your family makes proper financial decisions. *You* are the best person to look out for your family.

Financial Aid Gap or Unmet Need

It's worth repeating that the financial aid gap or unmet need refers to the missing amount of funds needed to attend a school. It could be the college aid offer does not cover your financial need as defined by federal law, or it could be the college has met this aid, but you feel your EFC was too high to begin with. In both cases, there is a gap in funding required to attend school. You might decide loans are a must. Some view a college loan no different than a car loan. Some people think debt is not a problem.

Debt upon Graduation

College financial statistics also tell you the average debt and the employment rate of graduating students. This helps to project a realistic picture of a student's financial situation upon graduation.

You may recall from the preface, my own daughter's solution to college expenses, "I'll just take a loan." She isn't alone in her thought process. She is the typical student, the one who assumes she can always pay this loan back.

In December 2010, CNBC aired *Price of Admission: America's College Debt Crisis.*[46] The documentary claimed America will face a student loan debt crisis. Just like in the housing market, loans are being approved for those who can't afford to borrow. Students believe repayment will be easy with a high salary job after graduation, but when high salary jobs are not always achieved students are defaulting on loans. This could be the next bail-out issue.

If someone claims your aid package is affordable, ask them to help you through these steps. Multiply the loans by four, which is a rough estimate (not including interest) of what the student will owe after graduation. Next, figure out in how many years and at what annual payment this loan will be paid off. Take this annual amount, add some annual rent, clothing, food and entertainment costs, and maybe a car loan, to arrive at the annual living expenses upon graduation. This is the *minimum* salary the student will be searching for when seeking employment. Is it reasonable?

Student loan repayment calculators can be found online and may also help project loan repayments and future salary needs.

---

46. CNBC, Price of Admission Video, http://www.cnbc.com/id/15840232? play=1&video=1719827701

You Decide What You Can Actually Afford

The government has come up with an amount that it expects you can pay toward college expenses, but it may feel inaccurate. The FAFSA doesn't account for income fluctuations. Maybe you don't receive a substantial bonus every year, or maybe there are some other reasons your EFC isn't reflected accurately.

Only you can decide what you can really afford. Review your budget, your income and expenses. Total four years of college expenses and divide that into monthly payments. Sometimes seeing "$500 a month" makes it very clear whether a school is affordable. If you think you can afford this figure, try it. Try putting this amount aside each month and see how life feels.

Choose an Affordable School

Students reapply for financial aid each year. There is no guarantee you will receive the same offer. In fact, if you are making withdrawals from excluded assets, you might be creating income, which guarantees you *less* aid next year. Students might just choose an affordable college to begin with; one you can pay for without any FAFSA aid. Choose this path and you eliminate all stress concerning EFC rules and any effect account withdrawals might have.

Choose the Military

When you don't have funds for college, the next best thing is for the student to be paid to go to college: attend an Academy, enter a Reserve Officer Training Corps (ROTC) program, or enlist to take advantage of all the education assistance offered. Students may need encouragement. I would never have attended USAFA if not for my brother's diligent persuasion and scrutiny over my application.

The military offers more than an education. Besides the pay and possible retirement at an early age, service members travel, and sometimes serving as little as two years provides health care *for life*. Veterans must meet required enlistment dates and restrictions and have served 24 continuous months or the full period for which they were called to active duty to qualify for VA health care.

Serving your country has both rewards and sacrifices. For details try *Military Education Benefits for College, A Comprehensive Guide for Military Members, Veterans, and Dependents* by Renza and Lizotte.

Plan a Transfer

Students could attend a community college for the first two years and then transfer to their choice school in order to graduate with the better diploma. This reduces college costs and is far better than entering a choice school that becomes unaffordable, and the student transfers to achieve a degree at a less prestigious school.

Try for Graduation in 3 Years or Double Major

Some high schools offer Advanced Placement (AP) classes or the International Baccalaureate (IB) program, an intense course load taken across junior and senior year. High scores on AP or IB exams sometimes qualify for college credits. Students might also test at their college for class validation.

The additional credit hours, plus a heavy semester workload or summer classes, can allow a student to meet college diploma requirements in only three years, saving thousands of dollars. Students who want the full four year college experience might still take this path to add a minor or double major to their degree.

Deciphering the Offer

As the student receives acceptance packages, each one should be analyzed to determine and compare the actual cost to the family. This means breaking out aid offers into free money, family funds, work-study, and loans. You are permitted to decline parts of aid packages. You could decline a loan and spend more student assets (*See* example p. 63). There are many elements in a college acceptance packet, some of which are discussed next.

Installment Plans

Ask if your college accepts installment plans. Instead of paying $10,000 up front, you can pay $1,000 a month over ten months. This works well when you pay expenses from your monthly income. If you pay your credit card in full each month, pay with a credit card instead of a check to receive frequent flyer miles, cash back, or whatever incentive program your card offers.

Remember, benefits are claimed when paid. Expenses for the first three months of the new calendar year, paid in the year prior, can only be used on the *prior year* tax return to claim benefits.

Scholarships

Scholarships are free money, usually based on academic, athletic, music, or some other type of performance. Many are restricted to be used for tuition and fees and some highly selective schools don't offer merit based scholarships at all. The acceptance packet will list any scholarships offered by the college. Scholarships can also be received from individual organizations.

The latest way to apply for scholarships often includes writing the essay live online. Please do not do this. Have students write and save all essays *on their home computer* so they can be easily edited and used again. Copy and paste the essay into the online form. There is nothing worse than hearing a student sent away a well written essay (using the online form) and now there is no record of its existence and no way to revise and use it again.

It's never too early to begin searching for scholarships. Some are even awarded in middle school. Online searches and even dated library books can be valuable since many scholarships are reoccurring. Two sites becoming popular are http://www.zinch. com (especially for niche scholarships such as skateboarding) and http://www.cappex.com (which is more merit based). Check for smaller scholarship amounts too. Remember, $1,000 is the same whether it's one award or ten scholarships of $100 each.

Parents should keep a file of scholarships received, restrictions on their use, who to contact when it's time to use the funds, and whether the funds will be paid directly to the school or to the student. Students might receive checks payable to themselves or payable to the college, in which case they must bring or forward the check to the school.

Make copies of all checks received for your expense folder so you have proof of receipt. School payments should be balanced with school expenses. Not only will this make tax filing easier, but you can be sure there are never any unused funds. You might find extra scholarship money was returned to an awarding organization and you must contact them to re-obtain the funds. In other cases, where schools received money directly, overpayments sit there, never returned or used. It could be an oversight, a mistake, or something as simple as missing a mailing address, but the point is you don't want it to be *your* scholarship money sitting there.

Ask whether a scholarship reoccurs and increases with inflation and find out if your school reduces gift aid, loans, or work-study when a scholarship is received.

Some schools might use a formula like:

| Cost of Attendance (COA) |
| - Expected Family Contribution (EFC) |
| - Aid From Other Sources (scholarships, relatives, etc.) |
| Student Financial Need |

Allocating scholarships like this does not reduce the EFC, so the family is still expected to pay the same amount. If possible, you would like the school to allocate the scholarship to reduce loans before work-study aid, but sometimes, the school has no choice:

> *Example:* A college COA is $10,000. A student received a $5,000 grant and $2,000 in scholarships to pay tuition and fees of $7,000. The student was also offered a $3,000 loan.

> This student wins a new scholarship of $1,000 restricted to tuition and fees. The school reallocates the figures to: a $4,000 grant, $3,000 in scholarships, and a $3,000 loan.

The student is upset because the loans did not decrease. The student feels like the scholarship was a waste of time; it saved the school $1,000. But, what could the school do? The scholarship had *restricted use,* to be allocated to tuition and fees. For this reason, students should look for scholarships with *non-restricted* use.

Anther situation can occur when a scholarship limit is reached.

> *Example:* A school offered a need-based grant for $6,000 to a student who also contributed an additional $1,000 (his EFC) from his after tax earnings. The student decides to quit working thinking, "I'll receive more aid."

> Now the student's need is $7,000 (because the student is not working) so the school offers the same $6,000 grant plus an additional $1,000 loan.

The student received more aid, but not free aid. If not working results in a loan, a loan the student has to repay with interest *by working,* maybe the student should just work to begin with.

One reason a school might do this is they have already reached the limit for the free aid allowance. In the case above, perhaps the school was only permitted to grant up to $6,000 in free aid. In this situation, the school has no more free aid to give, so of course, the additional aid is offered as a loan.

Campus-Based Aid—A Mix of Grants and Loans

Three need-based aid programs are run by the financial aid office at participating schools. Funds are *limited*. Every eligible student is not guaranteed to participate, nor do all schools offer all three types of programs. This shows why it's important to complete the FAFSA early. Each schools set it's own financial aid deadline, usually earlier than the FAFSA deadline.

> **Federal Supplemental Educational Opportunity Grant:** The Federal Supplemental Education Opportunity Grant (FSEOG) is a *need-based* grant that awards up to $4,000 depending on when you apply, school funding, if you're a Federal Pell Grant recipient, and your EFC amount.

> **Federal Perkins Loan:** A Perkins Loan is a *need-based* loan awarded by the school for up to $5,500 at a low 5 percent interest rate. There is a nine month grace period to begin repayments after graduation, drop-out, or if the student falls below half-time student status. (Not all schools participate.)

> **Federal Work-Study (FWS) Programs:** The FAFSA will ask if a student is interested in work-study. Students should always answer yes. Yes does not mean students have to work, but an answer of no means students may not be eligible to work even if they later change their mind. This work can be on or off campus at minimum wage (but sometimes higher). Students cannot earn more than their *need-based* work-study award amount and it is the student's responsibility to actually find the job. The student actually receives a paycheck, but work-study income isn't included on the FAFSA so it doesn't affect the EFC. Students should keep in mind, employment *means work*, it's not free aid, and the money received should be used for actual college expenses, not entertainment. (Parents may want to monitor how work-study money is spent.)

Grants

Grants are free (usually *need-based*) money. Each state has its own rules for state grant eligibility. Usually state grants cannot be used out-of-state or abroad, but check with your state to be sure. (Please check online for the current year amounts and rules to qualify.)

Federal Pell Grant

Pell grants are *need-based* grants derived from your Cost of Attendance (COA) and your FAFSA figures. They provide aid to *every* eligible student and can be used for more than tuition and fees.

The amount and qualifying factors can change from year to year. For example, in 2013-2014, the maximum award amount was $5,645 and your EFC had to be equal to or less than $5,081 (as compared to an EFC of $4,995 for the 2012-2013 Award Year).

Two additional grants possible for Pell eligible students are:

> **Academic Competitiveness Grant (ACG):** The Academic Competitiveness Grant provides $750 for the first year of study and $1,300 for the second year. The student *must be a Pell Grant* recipient and meet other criteria.

> **The National Science & Mathematics Access to Retain Talent Grant (National SMART Grant):** The SMART Grant awards up to $4,000 to undergraduates in their third and fourth year . Students *must be Pell eligible*, major in certain areas, and maintain a 3.0 GPA in coursework pertaining to the major.

Teacher Education Assistance for College and Higher Education (TEACH) Grant

The TEACH Grant, up to $4,000 each year, is *not need-based*. It is offered to students who intend to teach in elementary or secondary schools that serve students from low-income families.[47]

---

47. **Federal Student Aid**, *TEACH Grant Program,* http://studentaid.ed.gov/ PORTALSWebApp/students/english/TEACH.jsp

Loans

Loans offer students the opportunity to attend college, but they also award debt. Completing the FAFSA four times means four possible loans, or eight loans, if loans are taken per semester. This does not help a student's credit rating.

Some people think loans are a must and view college loans as no different than car loans, but in general, loans should be avoided. You can find plenty of reasons not to take a loan and even more reasons not to co-sign on a loan at http://studentloanjustice.org.

At some point, you might hear students jokingly refer to their student loans as my cruise, my boat, or my country cottage. What they mean is, "Had I not taken that loan, I would have gone on a cruise, owned a boat, or purchased a country cottage."

Usually, loan is not *good debt*. Good debt is debt that allows you to make money elsewhere. Good debt might be a house, where you owe a mortgage (the debt) but the house appreciates (hopefully) and you make money. Good debt is a credit card offer to write a cash advance check at zero percent interest for twelve months with no service charge. Good debt is borrowing on margin to make money in the stock market.

A loan may be good debt if you aim to keep investment gains off your tax return. Take a low interest loan to avoid selling your investment in base years. (Assets held are assessed at 5.64%, but once sold become income possibly assessed at 47%. *See* p.54)

But, loans aren't even debt with collateral. If you buy a car and change your mind, you can resell the car. If you overspend on a house, even in the worst case, the house is there to offset the loan in a foreclosure. College is also a purchase, but when you decide this college isn't going to work and have already spent $10,000, there is no collateral to offset this debt. Actually, this isn't quite accurate. The debt can and will be offset through garnishments, seizing of assets, and other areas not considered when the loan was taken.

If students ignore these cautions, take a loan and begin to fall behind on repayments, they should contact the lender to explore options. Usually a loan can be extended, which means more payments over a longer period of time, which means more interest, but at least the students' credit rating would stay intact.

Students might also qualify for Loan Repayment Assistance Programs (LRAP) to receive assistance if they do public service work or work in areas with unmet needs. Generally, when a loan is forgiven, the cancelled amount must be reported as taxable income, but forgiveness under LRAP is tax-free.

Stafford Loan

As of 2010, the U.S. government is the lender for Stafford loans.

Subsidized Stafford Loan: The Subsidized Stafford Loan is a *need-based* loan that ranges in amount depending on grade level and degree. No interest is charged while the student is in school and undergraduate rates were as low as 3.86 percent for 2013-2014. Learn more at http://www.staffordloan.com/stafford-loan-info/

Unsubsidized Loan: This loan is *not need-based* and the interest accumulates while in school but no payment is due until after graduation. The interest rate is 3.86 percent.

Parent Loans for Undergraduate Students (PLUS) Loans

Plus loans are available for the total Cost Of Attendance less any aid awarded. They are *not need-based* and offered at a rate of 6.41 percent (for 2013-2014) to parents of all income levels who have good credit.

Credit Card Loans (Advances)

If your credit card offers a convenience check with a zero percent interest rate for twelve months, *and* the processing fee beats other loan rates, *and* you can make full monthly repayments completed by the deadline, you might consider it. Ask ahead what happens if you miss a payment. Sometimes you incur interest from the date the convenience check was originally cashed (maybe 11 months back). Do *not* cash a convenience check under these terms.

International Schools

Federal aid can be used for study abroad programs run through U.S. schools. When the school is actually a foreign school, complete the FAFSA, but also contact the school's financial aid office to see if they can award aid in accordance to federal rules. Also look for scholarships that are eligible to be used abroad.

College Cost & College Offer Worksheets

Estimate and compare college costs. Enter the college information
and any aid the student is offered (*See also* Example p. 131).

College Cost Worksheet	Example *(See p. 131)*	College 1	College 2
A) COA	$28,335		
B) EFC	$ 5,000		
C) Your Need (COA − EFC = Need)	$23,335		
D) Percent of Need Met by School	79%	%	%
E) Estimated aid to receive from the school (E = C × D)	$18,435		
F) *Free aid:* Percent of Free aid allocated by the school	32%	%	%
G) Free aid the student can expect to receive (G = E × F)	$5,899		
H) *Self-help aid:* Percent of Self-help aid allocated by the school	68%	%	%
I) Self-help aid the student expects to receive (I = E × H)	$12,536		
J) Unmet Need (J = C − G − I)	$ 4,900		
K) Amount Family Must Pay (including loans and work-study) (K = B + I + J)	$22,436		
L) Years of college	× 4 yrs	× 4 yrs	× 4 yrs
M) *Total College Cost (M = K × L)	$89,744		
N) *Monthly Cost *(while in college)* N = (B+ J) ÷ 12 months	$ 825		

*Interest is not included. This sheet provides a rough estimate to
show unmet need, how assistance is allocated between free and
self-help aid, the total college cost, and the monthly payment
(not including work-study or loans) a family must make.

Compare College Offers

Calculate unmet need and compare free and self-help aid offers.

Comparing Offers & Calculating Unmet Need	Interest Rate	College 1	College 2
COA			
−EFC			
A) Your Financial Need			
Free Aid / Gift Aid			
Pell Grant (amt:_____)			
ACG (amt:_____)			
SMART Grant (amt:___)			
TEACH Grant (up to $4,000)			
State Grant			
Private Scholarships			
School Grant or Scholarship			
FSEOG (up to $4,000)			
B) Your Total *Free* Aid:			
Loans (self-help aid)			
Perkins Loan (amt:_____)	___%		
Stafford Subsidized Loan (amt:_____)	___%		
Stafford Unsubsidized Loan (amt:_____)	___%		
PLUS Loan (up to COA amount)	___%		
Credit Card Advance (up to credit card limit)	___%		
C) Your Total *Loan* Aid:			
Work-Study (self-help aid)			
D) Your *Work-Study* Award			
Unmet Need = A - B - C - D			

What is Professional Judgment (PJ)?

Financial Aid Advisors at the schools are allowed to use Professional Judgment (PJ) in certain circumstances.

The following are examples of changes that might be made:

a. "Also, you may use professional judgment (PJ) to adjust the income line items to reflect income the family receives that doesn't appear on the tax return."[48]

— This might be done when a family's tax write-offs create a zero or negative income.

b. Adjust income lines to add an amount to untaxed income in cases where students receive support not accounted for on the FAFSA.[49]

— FAAs might also adjust the room and board component of Cost of Attendance (COA) for a student who receives in-kind support (such as receiving a free room at a relative's or friend's house)

c. Create dependency overrides to change a student's status from dependent to independent student (but not the reverse).[50]

The first two actually work against the student. The student will receive less aid. They are accomplished in the interest of keeping things fair. For example, the student receiving free room and board should need less aid than the student who pays for this expense. Overriding a dependency will help students with unique situations qualify for more aid.

48. Application and Verification Guide, *Filling out the FAFSA,* "Zero Income," http://ifap.ed.gov/fsahandbook/attachments/1314FSAHandbookCompleteActiveIndex.pdf

49. Ibid, "Independent Student with Parental Support Example,"

50. Ibid. "Dependency Overrides,".

Appealing an Offer

When an aid offer is received, you can question it further. This is sometimes referred to as negotiating the offer, but try not to use this word with Financial Aid Advisors. The base year is the most important as it sets your financial picture for future years. Sometimes funds are reserved for four years based on your incoming year.

There may be times when you can negotiate for greater aid. Consider contacting the college and discussing the following:

1. A dependency override is needed for unique circumstances

2. If your research on the college shows a typical aid package receives more aid than yours, ask why.

3. If two colleges of similar Cost of Attendance offer you significantly different aid packages, ask why.

    — Federal aid is fairly straight forward, by applying a formula, so the schools themselves should also be interested in differences in awards.

4. If your income will be significantly different next year due to a bonus received, overtime worked, a job lost, or a second job that was only temporary, notify the school.

5. You could point out that you live in one state and work in another, so the State and Other Tax Allowance is skewed.

6. The cost of living in your area of the country is not considered in EFC calculations, so you could save receipts to show Financial Aid Advisors that the Income Protection Allowance is too low for where you live.

7. You might demonstrate unusual expenses by discussing:

    a. Tuition you pay for siblings' school

    b. The increased cost for a sibling who is changing from public to private school in the upcoming year

    c. Unusual medical and dental expenses

    d. Parents' education expenses, if attending school

Personal Judgment can be used to adjust aid, but don't count on it. At the same time, don't skip mentioning your concerns because you just never know if it will make a difference. Always ask.

Increase Aid and Reduce Debt

The following list isn't all-inclusive, nor is it a direct summary of all the strategies discussed in this book. It is a brief list of items to consider when trying to increase aid and cut debt. It is important to read the entire book to be clear on the logic behind an idea and the EFC rule it is targeting.

Each idea is also relevant to your own personal circumstances. Some ideas are aimed at meeting the special EFC categories. Some are aimed at shielding assets (which not everyone needs to do) and some aim at reducing income. Not every idea will work for your family. Please do *not* read this as a list *everyone* should do.

Consider for the New Baby

1. Open a ten-pay whole life insurance plan (insuring the baby) at a dividend paying participating mutual company.

2. Save in a 529 Plan owned by the parents.

3. Create earned income for the baby to contribute to a Roth IRA. Try modeling work for a local or family business, or when older, let the child work as a household employee.

Relatives Might Consider

1. Opening a 529 plan in their name with the student as the beneficiary, with the intention to assist with the senior year of college, preferably after the last FAFSA submission.

2. Gifts of Series EE/I Bonds in the parents' name with the child as the beneficiary.

3. Giving monetary gifts to the parent prior to base years so it only counts as an asset, not income.

4. Contributing to Roth IRAs for employed students.

5. Giving monetary gifts to the student after college (not during college when it counts as money received).

6. Opening a ten-pay whole life insurance policy (insuring themselves or the student) at a dividend paying participating mutual company.

High School Students Might

1. Begin a student resume as early as freshman year of high school listing achievements and ideas that might be used when applying to college or for scholarships.

2. Maintain grades and apply for merit based scholarships.

3. Aim to graduate college in less than four years. Take high school classes that might count for college credit.

4. Consider entering the military.

5. Consider attending a community college for the first year or two and then transfer to a dream school.

6. Distinguish between college education and entertainment expenses and cut the entertainment.

7. Politely appeal an aid package and ask for a Professional Judgment Adjustment for unique circumstances.

Income and Assets

1. Work in places that offer employee scholarships (McDonalds, Burger King, Walmart, etc.).

2. Run a Google search for Fast Food Scholarships. You may not have to be employed there to apply (KFC, Starbucks, Dunkin Donuts, and more).

3. Start a business (tutoring, eBay, Zazzle.com, elderly help, web page design, freelance writing or photography, etc.)

4. Save paychecks in a Roth IRA if employed.

5. Stop working once student income approaches the student Total Allowances deducted from income.

6. Avoid taking a year off to work since a full time salary will increase the student EFC.

7. Spend all their assets (student money) first, before parents' assets and before signing the FAFSA.

8. Spend down custodial accounts and trusts or try to roll them over into 529 Plans.

Aiming at the Automatic Zero EFC or Simplified Needs Test

1. If the parents' income is near $50,000 or $24,000, review prior year taxes to see if entries can be manipulated to reduce the AGI below these thresholds (2014-2015 rules).

2. Review all the components included in your income to see if they can be reduced and also see if you can increase any of the elements for the allowances deducted from income.

3. Try to qualify for government assistance programs (like Reduced Price School Lunch, SNAP (Food Stamps), etc.).

4. Don't file a Form 1040 if you can file the Form 1040A or 1040EZ. You qualify for the Automatic Zero EFC and SNT if you are *eligible* to file a form 1040A or 1040EZ, but filing the 1040 when you are not required, only creates scrutiny and questions from Financial Aid Advisors.

5. Don't do things that *require* you to file a Form 1040. Consider not itemizing, not selling stocks (avoid the Schedule D), avoiding Health Savings Account (HSA) withdrawals and arranging to delay receipt of alimony. Avoid anything that requires filing the Form 1040. (Filing the 1040 solely to claim education credits is permitted. It does not disqualify you from qualifying for the special EFC categories.)

6. When you have a choice, claim an expense on the front of the Form 1040 instead of itemizing it.

7. Consider choosing the Tuition and Fees Deduction instead of education credits if it is needed to qualify you for the Automatic Zero or SNT. Otherwise, choose the education credits, if eligible.

8. Be careful liquidating educational accounts or other investments that might result in an increased AGI.

9. Consider contributing to an Traditional IRA or employer plan and/or start a self-employed retirement plan such as a Simplified Employee Pension Plan (SEP) or Savings Incentive Match Plan for Employees (SIMPLE) plan.

10. Consider the list of items parents might do, including their homes, investments, and taxes. Many of these items will reduce your Adjusted Gross Income (AGI) (*See p. 149*)

Self-employed or Small Business Owners Might

1. Hire a nonworking spouse in the family business to reduce profit and take advantage of the Employment Expense Allowance.

2. Hire the children in the family business to decrease profit and create earned income for a student Roth IRA.

3. Reduce AGI by claiming health insurance premiums on the *front* of Form 1040 (line 28), instead of itemizing.

4. Decrease self-employment profit by grouping expenses in the same year; buy supplies in bulk or replace equipment.

Parents Might

1. Estimate your EFC *and* expected aid offer for each college, and plan the FAFSA signing date to reflect the most need.

2. Save only in your (the parents') name.

3. Cancel the lawn service; mow and rake leaves yourself.

4. Cancel a gym membership; exercise at home or try running.

5. If a sibling is approaching college as well, let the older student take a year off perhaps to volunteer abroad, so both students will attend college at the same time.

6. Spend money from included assets now (that you planned to spend anyway on home repair, airline tickets, etc.) or pay off debts (credit cards, car loan, medical bills, etc.).

7. Forgo a loan if you have EFC "included" assets to spend.

8. Only pull loans from insurance or retirement accounts.

9. Have a nonworking spouse obtain part-time work since 35 percent of the income (*up to $4,000*) will be shielded by the Employment Expense Allowance.

10. If employed at a college, have your student attend that college for two to four years, to take advantage of tuition discounts offered to children of employees.

11. If divorced, separated, or a single parent, consider how assets should be split, who should own any educational accounts, and who should have custody in the base years.

Parents' Home(s)

1. Don't relocate if you will lose the opportunity for state aid.

2. Consider buying a house (primary residence) to build equity shielded from the federal formula.

3. Consider prepaying your mortgage with money from included assets.

4. Consider a home equity line of credit from a secondary residence to pay off other debts.

5. Consider making your second home a rental property, requiring completion of a Schedule E on your tax return.

6. Begin a rental property business by purchasing a house near the college, renting to your student plus some roommates. If it operates as a loss, deduct it on the Form 1040.

Parents' Investments

1. Invest in accounts that only increase in share price; avoid interest, dividends, and capital gains in base year AGIs.

2. If you can't avoid dividends and capital gains, consider selling a loser stock to offset these gains and reduce AGI.

3. Consider borrowing on margin, rather than selling stocks to pay expenses. There will be no impact to your AGI.

4. Consider taking a loan before selling investments to take advantage of low interest rates and avoid gains on your tax return. Stocks held are assessed at 5.64% but once sold become income assessed at a max of 47% (*See* p. 54).

5. Save in retirement accounts. Remember IRAs can be done for both parents, even when only one is employed.

6. Use IRAs for investments that distribute capital gains or dividends, so growth will not impact your tax return.

7. Consider purchasing whole life insurance plans.

8. Consider investing in educational savings accounts, especially if you can't qualify for educational tax benefits.

9. Consider EE/I bonds when you want to save with no restrictions on how the money will be used.

Parents' Taxes

1. Review all the components included in your income to see if they can be reduced and also see if you can increase any of the elements for the allowances deducted from income.

2. File your taxes early for easier FAFSA completion and your assets will decrease from the filing fee and any taxes owed.

3. Sign the FAFSA after gaining a new dependent (such as in cases of adoption or perhaps remarriage to a nonworking spouse) and before someone's imminent death.

4. Don't file your return with a Kiddie Tax on it, but instead file separate returns for each child.

5. Watch student loans and student income so they don't remove parents' eligibility for the dependency exemption.

6. Defer a bonus from work or postpone jury duty to keep this additional income off your tax return in base years.

7. Avoid the Schedule D. Cash investment accounts with gains after the FAFSA is signed for senior year of college (assuming no siblings are in or approaching college).

8. Consider starting a business. New businesses create self-employment taxes and usually operate at a loss in the early years, both of which reduce AGI. They can also employ the student and create earned income for an IRA.

9. Plan for all medical expenses to occur in one year; preferably not in base years. Higher taxes reduce your EFC.

10. If you are a teacher, claim all your Educator Expenses on the front of the Form 1040, (line 23).

11. Create moving expenses by moving to a new location, preferably within your state to continue to qualify for state aid. (You must meet IRS rules concerning new job requirements to be eligible to claim moving expenses.)

12. Check if the tax benefits you receive by selling education investments (EE/I Bonds, 529 Plans, etc.) outweigh their impact on increasing your AGI which increases your EFC.

13. Consider who can and should claim education tax benefits.

14. Use the tax refund to pay for college.

Ideas for Students in College

1. Apply for scholarships every year and don't forget to check nonprofit organizations, especially local ones.

2. Don't take on a pet.

3. Don't pay for haircuts; have a friend cut the student's hair.

4. Ask about school voucher programs (financial assistance).

5. Buy used or rent textbooks.

6. Buy less clothing and shop at thrift stores.

7. Hang laundry to dry, reducing the electric bill.

8. Cancel cable TV and use an antenna or a laptop for TV.

9. Use campus childcare if needed.

10. Cancel the home phone and keep just the cell phone, or better yet, cancel the cell phone.

11. Forgo a gym membership and utilize the free campus gym.

12. Ask if there is a student discount every time something is paid for (consider restaurants, haircuts, tax returns, bus passes, museum access, newspaper delivery, etc.)

Transportation and Entertainment

1. Carpool and fill the tank when gasoline prices are low.

2. Purchase a bike instead of a car or use the bus and campus transportation instead of driving.

3. Combine errands into one trip, even one weekly trip.

4. Stop paying for movies; use the library to rent a movie.

5. Give away or sell the game box and games; earn income in the resulting free time.

6. Skip the vacation or check the institutions community service office for last minute deals.

7. Volunteer at a far away place to get a vacation for free.

Food

1. Skip purchasing a microwave for the dorm room.

2. Stop eating out, including the quick coffee trips.

3. Stop in to visit nearby relatives at dinner time and be happy to take leftovers; do laundry while there.

4. Work at restaurants that provide free food for employees.

5. Have a party where everyone brings a dish. Keep the leftovers.

6. Clip coupons or search for coupons online.

7. Pay attention to local brands when grocery shopping.

8. Prepare meals for the entire week ahead of time and prepare enough for leftovers (saving time and money).

Income and Taxes

1. Move money into excluded assets.

2. Become employed: try waiting tables, bartending, or transcribing, but don't sacrifice grades for a job.

3. Babysit the professors' kids or pets.

4. Consider only working in the summer.

5. Look for ads that pay for participating in interviews, medical tests, surveys, etc., offered by companies or by students working on a masters or other project.

6. Start a business (freelance writing, photography, eBay selling, consulting, or teach the elderly to use the internet).

7. Sell used items (CDs, books, clothes) online or to thrift stores or Half-Price Books.

8. Contribute any saved earned income to a Roth IRA.

9. Watch for adds for free tax filing.

10. Claim an education tax credit—if it is more beneficial than claiming it on the parents' return. (The student dependent exemption would be unclaimed.)

Abbreviations

ACGs: Academic Competitiveness Grants
AGI: Adjusted Gross Income
AI: Available Income
AAI: Adjusted Available Income
AVG: Application and Verification Guide
COA: Cost of Attendance
CPS: Central Processing System
DOMA: Defense of Marriage Act
DRN: Data Release Number
EFC: Expected Family Contribution
EIN: Employer Identification Number
ESA: Education Savings Account
FAA: Financial Aid Administrator
FAFSA: Free Application for Federal Student Aid
FM: Federal Methodology
FOTW: FAFSA on the web
FSAIC: Federal Student Aid Information Center
FWS: Federal Work-Study
HEA: Higher Education Act
HEOA: Higher Education Opportunity Act
HUD: Housing and Urban development
IM: Institutional Methodology
IPA: Income Protection Allowances
ISIR: Institutional Student Information Record
IRA: Individual Retirement Account
NSLDS: National Student Loan Data System
PC: Parent Contribution
PIN: Personal Identification Number
PJ: Professional Judgment
QTP: Qualified Tuition Program (Also called Section 529 Plans)
SAR: Student Aid Report
SAC: Student Asset Contribution
SIC: Student Income Contribution
SNT: Simplified Needs Test
TEACH: Teachers Education Assistance for College
UGMA: Uniform Gift to Minor Act
UTMA: Uniform Transfers to Minor Act
WIA: Workforce Investment Act

Resources

Internet addresses often change. Please notify us if an Internet Uniform Resource Locator (URL) referenced is no longer found.

To received additional recommendations visit:
http://www.kidsandmoneytoday.com/subscribe/

Calculators (for understanding growth)

1. A simple compound interest calculator can be found at http://www.moneychimp.com/calculator/compound_interest_calculator.htm

2. An annual return calculator for a portfolio is found at http://www.mymoneyblog.com/estimate-your-portfolios-rate-of-return-calculator.html.

3. A calculator for comparing one year to the next can be found at http://www.mathsisfun.com/money/compound-interest-calculator.html. This calculator will find the unknown when you have three of the following four factors: rate, period, present value, and future value.

Calculators (for student loan repayment)

1. Federal Student Aid http://www.direct.ed.gov/calc.html

2. The Smart Guide to Financial Aid, Loan Calculator at http://www.finaid.org/calculators/loanpayments.phtml

College Research

1. At http://www.collegeboard.com, if you enter a school in the college search box and click *Cost and Financial Aid,* you will pull up the school's financial statistics.

2. Also try the Department of Education's College Navigator found at http://nces.ed.gov/collegenavigator

FAFSA & EFC Resources (*See* p. 9)

Federal School Codes
The Federal School Codes list is found at: https://fafsa.ed.gov/FAFSA/app/schoolSearch?locale=en_EN

Financial Planning Books (further reading)

1. *Debt-Free U: How I Paid for an Outstanding College Education Without Loans, Scholarships, or Mooching off My Parents*, by Zac Bissonnette and Andrew Tobias, 2010

2. *Deduct It!: Lower Your Small Business Taxes* by Stephen Fishman J.D., 2010

3. *The Kid's ROTH IRA Handbook: Securing Tax-Free Wealth From a Child's First Paycheck or Money Answers for Employed Children, Their Parents, the Self-Employed and Entrepreneurs* by Tracy Foote, 2008

4. *Military Education Benefits for College: A Comprehensive Guide for Military Members, Veterans, and Their Dependents*, by David Renza & Edmund Lizotte, 2010

5. *Parlay Your IRA into a Family Fortune: 3 EASY STEPS for creating a lifetime supply of tax-deferred, even tax-free, wealth for you and your family*, Ed Slott, 2008

6. *Paying for College without Going Broke*, by Princeton Review and Kalman A. Chany, 2009

7. *Pay for College without Sacrificing Your Retirement: A Guide to Your Financial Future*, by Tim Higgins, 2008

Social Media
Connect with us:
   Facebook:
     Click like at: http://Facebook.com/KidsAndMoneyToday

   Twitter
     Follow at: http://Twitter.com/KidsMoneyToday

   YouTube
     Subscribe at: http://Youtube.com/KidsAndMoneyToday

   Google+: Follow at
     https://plus.google.com/+Kidsandmoneytoday/posts

   Book Updates
     View updates to this book at:
     http://www.kidsandmoneytoday.com/FAFSA-Education/

Index

Does your student have a Roth IRA yet?

Imagine if every child had a Roth IRA...

Let's leave better children for the world.

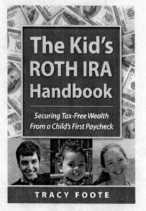

1. *Money Management:* Appreciate the benefits of a Roth IRA

2. *Career Skills:* Identify different types of child employment

3. *New Ideas:* Discover different ways parents can employ their children

4. *Introduction to Taxes:* Basic tax concepts for children with low earned income

5. *Powerful Knowledge:* Understand rules for children to contribute to a Roth IRA.

Available for purchase at http://Amazon.com

Have you started your business YouTube channel?

1. *Prioritize:* Create videos based on analytical business objectives

2. *Targeted Traffic:* Identify your customer, how they search, and how to be found

3. *Conversions:* Prepare videos to meet your monetization goals

4. *Social Media Strategies:* Share properly to increase sales

5. *Analytics:* Quick start to basic tracking methods including plugins, Google Analytics, and YouTube Analytics

Available for purchase at http://Amazon.com

Review Request

If you would recommend *How You Can Maximize Student Aid* to others, please consider writing a 5 star review on Amazon.com.

How to write a review in 4 easy steps:

1. On the Internet visit http://www.Amazon.com
2. Enter 0-9814737-4-1 in the search box on Amazon
3. About half way down, click *Create Your Own Review*
4. Please tell others what you liked about this book

Reader Comments and Inquiries

Comments, inquiries, or documented updates should be emailed to http://KidsAndMoneyToday.com/contact/. All remarks are considered for future editions and/or website updates to further assist readers.

To view updated family finance tips about kids and money visit:

http://KidsAndMoneyToday.com/subscribe/

Easily Order this Book for a Friend

- at your local bookstore
- from the publisher at http://www.TracyTrends.com
- online from Amazon.com at:
  http://www.amazon.com/exec/obidos/ASIN/0981473741/

CPSIA information can be obtained at www.ICGtesting.com
Printed in the USA
BVOW05s2127221014

371937BV00001B/107/P